Adam!

Where Are You?

Why Most Black Men Don't Go to Church

by Jawanza Kunjufu

Dedication

To all African American males who have not confessed Jesus Christ as Lord, I say to you: The Lord stands at the door to your heart and knocks. If you would only believe that Christ is real, that He died for you, that your sins have been washed away, and that He's coming back for you, He will give you a peace that transcends all understanding and a joy that is truly indescribable!

To pastors and fellow believers, my prayer is that you will search within your souls and design churches and develop ministries that will be influential in bringing African American males to Christ.

Acknowledgments

I thank God for a praying grandmother (Cecil Prisentine), parents who took me to church, my pastor Jeremiah A. Wright, Jr. who reflects the African essence of Christian manhood, and a wife who has placed God, through Jesus Christ as the head of her life.

FOREWORD

When God asked the question, "Where are you, Adam?" in the first book of the Bible, several factors made the listening audience 5000 years ago a lot different from the reading audience at the end of the 20th Century. First of all, the listening audience who first heard this story understood clearly that God already knew where the man (*adamah*) was. The problem was that the man did not know where he was.

Unfortunately, the circumstances are the same today as they were when this sacred story was first told. God knows where the black man is. The black man -- who is still trying to hide from God -- is the one who does not know where he is -- even though he *thinks* he knows. Even more tragic, however, is the fact that although the *circumstances* are the same, the *awareness* is not!

That is to say that the listening audience in 3000 B.C. understood that God knew. They were aware that God knew painfully and poignantly where the man was; but the reading audience in the 1990s does not understand. For the most part they were not aware that God knows where the black man is even when the black man (who *thinks* he knows) in reality *does* not know!

The first difference, therefore, between the listening audience and the reading audience is the subtle nuance of irony that is implicit in the question raised by God with the man. The next difference exacerbates the nature of the tragedy. The listening audience 5000 years ago was primarily *male!* Men were the ones who heard, who studied and loved *TORAH*, and this question comes from the first book of Torah.

Today the reading audience is primarily female -- especially when it comes to the reading audience who would be reading (or hearing sermons preached about) the book of Genesis, and God's question to the couple in Paradise. Where it was understood back then that "the congregation of the righteous" (to quote Psalm One) was made up primarily of men and secondarily of women, that is *not* the understanding now. In fact, just the opposite is the case.

That is one of the reasons why Dr. Kunjufu's work is so important! He addresses some hard questions to help the reader understand the drastic and dramatic shift from a people of faith then who were Black and male to a people of faith now who are predominately female -- especially among the descendants of the same Black people whose faith was at the outset. What has caused Black men who were once proud to be men of faith, to be so visibly absent from "the congregation of the righteous"?

We have moved from a time when Black men were in the majority in congregations, through a time when men were the plurality in most congregations, to the present when men are a pitiful minority in most Black congregations. When surveying the six historic Black denominations that have memberships in the United States of over 2 million each, C. Eric Lincoln and Lawrence Mamiya point out in their classic work *(The Black Experience in Religion)* that there is a movement of African American men away from Christianity toward Islam. What has caused this male "exodus" from the Black church over the last 2000 years?

When one reads the history of the African American Church in North America -- especially that period during the 18th and 19th Centuries famous names of brave, bold, bodacious Black men jump off the pages and confront the reader. Names like Richard Allen, Absalom Jones, Peter Varick, Alexander Crummel, Bishop Henry McNeal Turner, Edward Wilmot Blyden, Rev. Gabriel Prosser (the Baptist minister who led the African revolt in 1800), Denmark Vesey, Rev. Nathaniel Turner, Rev. Morris Brown, and William Seymore ... names like these pepper the pages of our history.

Strong Black men banded together under the banner of Jesus Christ to throw off the yoke of slavery, and in this period the number of Black men in the congregation (percentage wise) were four times what they are today. Black men who were Christians were much more likely to have what Cornel West calls "a combative spirituality." And remember: this is 100 to 150 years before the appearance of W.D. Fard, Elijah Poole (later Elijah Muhammed) or Nobel Drew Ali!

Christian men like Marcus Garvey saw no contradiction between being free, being Black and being followers of Christ.

The numbers of black men in black churches swelled under the clarion call of Him who said "If the Son shall set you free, you shall be free indeed!" What happened between those days and this day to make God ask once again, "Adam? Where *are* you? Black man? Where *are* you?" Why have our Black men dwindled in numbers and disappeared from the pews where they were once our leaders and our warriors?

Is it racism? Is it Europeanized Christianity? Is it Euro-centric theology and Renaissance art? Is it the Nation of Islam? Is it orthodox Islam? Is it the mis-teaching of Scripture and Church History or what Carter G. Woodson called "the miseducation of the Negro?" Is it what Dr. James Washington of Union Theological Seminary in New York calls "the bourgeoisification of the black church?" Is it what Cornel West calls "cultural hybridization?" Is it the lack of what Molefi Asante argues for: a conceptual framework that speaks more readily to the history, culture and theology of African Americans? Or is it a combination of all of the above?

These are the questions Dr. Kunjufu tackles in this much-needed work, and these are the questions I urge you to take seriously as you work on the solutions to this historical tragedy. The question God asked in the first book of Scripture was based in a culture that was steeped in the symbols and meanings of the faith.

Our culture, on the other hand, is highly secular, highly technological and highly arrogant. Our post-Enlightenment, post-modern and self-sufficient mindset tells us many things that we need to *unlearn* if we are ever to reappropriate a level of spiritually that produced the Great Text that raised the question which still haunts -- *Black Man? Where Are You?*

Chancellor Williams and Judge R. Eugene Pincham serve as philosophical polarities which should guide your slow and thoughtful reading of Dr. Kunjufu's work. Chancellor Williams warns us not to forget "our story." In repeating the legend of Sumer, he says the traveler asked the old man, "What happened to the people of Sumer? History teaches us that they were black! Where are they? What happened to them?"

"Ah," sighed the old man, "They forgot their story (their history) and so they died." We need to *remember* our history, *remember* our story and *retell* our story to our children as

Moses warned us, or we too will continue to die.

R. Eugene Pincham, a retired judge from the Illinois Appellate Court once said, "You can't *be* what you can't *see!*" One of the reasons so many of our young, African American brothers grow up "antichurch" and not wanting to be a part of the church -- beyond the pressures of the peer group -- is that they "can't see" strong African American men *in* church, as a part of the church, *loving* the church, *supporting* the church, *tithing* to the church, building up the church and *being* the church -- outside of the church building.

Once they begin to see that, and once we begin to tell our story, the question that God asks the man (*adamah*) will begin to have a different answer. We can move from hiding behind fig leaves to rebuilding our families and our communities as "priests" in our homes! Dr. Kunjufu is to be commended for this work, and you are to be commended for reading it and implementing its positive solutions.

> Rev. Dr. Jeremiah A. Wright, Jr.
> Trinity United Church of Christ
> Chicago, IL

Introduction

I have thought for a long time about why most African American males don't go to church. However I never thought about writing a book.

Then the Lord inspired me to write this book and I can always tell when the Lord is in charge, because I'm not controlling the process. This book was written in five days! One day to categorize my ideas into chapter outline form and four days to write. To God be the Glory!

Genesis 3:8-10

Then the man and his wife heard the sound of the Lord God as He was walking in the garden in the cool of the day, and they hid from the Lord God among the trees of the garden. But the Lord God said to the man, "Where are you?" He answered, "I heard you in the garden and I was afraid because I was naked; so I hid."

Why does Adam believe he can hide from God? Was God's question, "Where are you Adam?" a rhetorical question? Did God know where Adam was all the time? Why is God so concerned about Adam? Why would Adam be afraid if he heard God? Why is Adam afraid of being naked in the eyes of God?

The Garden of Eden story takes place in Africa. The Pishon river is the White Nile and the Gihon river is the Blue Nile. They flow through the Garden of Eden. Archaeologist document that human life began in Africa approximately four million years ago. In African theology the Trinity was Ausar, Aset, and Heru. The Greek trinity is Osiris, Isis, and Horus. The present trinity is Father, Son, and Holy Spirit. African mythology teaches that Osiris represented the best in African manhood. He was killed by his brother Set, or Satan. His wife Isis was distraught and vowed to resurrect her husband. His body was broken into fourteen pieces and she was able to reclaim all of his parts. She created a phallic symbol in his honor that the Greeks called an obelisk; the Africans called it tekhen. This phallic symbol is shown in America as the Washington monument. This symbol also exists in London, Paris, and Rome. (I wonder whether they know they are paying homage to the resurrection of Adam, the Black man!)

Anecdotes

What happens when a son watches his father read the Bible and pray?

Have Black men transferred their anger from their earthly father to their Heavenly father?

How can Black men holler more for Jordan than Jesus?

When you separate a Black man from God, you strip him from his power.

When you save a Black man, you save a Black family.

TABLE OF CONTENTS

CHAPTER 1

Searching For Adam

It was a bright and sunny Sunday morning; Mrs. Fuller had already begun preparing Sunday breakfast-pancakes, turkey sausage, scrambled eggs, and orange juice. Her fourteen year-old daughter was helping her, and gospel music was playing in the background. Mrs. Fuller and Renee seemed to have the grace to flip over pancakes without ever missing a beat on each song. It was a very cheerful day in the Fuller household on this Sunday morning, and they were grateful that the Lord had given them one more day. They realized that it was the Lord, and not the alarm clock, that woke them up that morning and they were singing His praises on this beautiful Lord's day.

The twin boys, Wayne and David, were as usual still in bed this morning. They had gone out to a party the night before and did not get home until 2:30 in the morning. Mrs. Fuller asked Renee, "Do you think your brothers will be going to church this morning?" Renee said, "I'm sure David will be going because his girlfriend is singing in the choir." Mrs. Fuller then decided that since the boys are not going to get up on their own, she would go up to their room and, as a normal Sunday morning ritual, she would try to convince them that they needed to be in the house of the Lord. She tells Renee to watch the food as she ascends the steps still humming the Sounds of Blackness' latest hit, "If You Believe." She smiles as she goes up the steps because she realizes that, if she is going to get Wayne and David to go to church, she is definitely going to have to exercise her faith; after all, faith is the

1

substance of things hoped for, the evidence of things unseen.

She opens the door of their room and exclaims, "It's time to get up, Wayne and David!" Wayne slowly opens his eyes and says, "Ah, Ma, do you know what time it is? We didn't get in until 2:30, and you know I need more than six hours of sleep." She responds, "If you can party on Saturday night, then you surely can be in the house of the Lord on Sunday morning."

"You don't understand Ma, I'm sleepy and I'm tired, and it would make no sense for me to go to church and fall asleep. Besides, I don't really understand what's going on in the church anyway." Mrs. Fuller replies, "You never will understand if you don't go, and if you cannot stay awake. Did you fall asleep at the party last night, and did you understand all the words of the rap music that was played last night? I think it would be easier to understand the sermon than to understand what is said on those rap cassettes that you listened to last night."

David begins to stir ever so slightly. "How you doing, Ma?" "I'm doing okay, Baby. Are you going to church with us this morning?" she asks. David began to loosen the sleep out of his eyes and says, "Yeah, I'm going Ma." She then asks, "David, are you going because you want to go?" Wayne quickly butts in saying, "Naw, he ain't going cause he wants to go; he's going because his girlfriend is singing in the choir." David then rebuts, "It doesn't matter why I'm going; what matters is that I'm getting up and I am going to church, which is more than I can say for you." As David gets out of the bed and goes to the washroom, his mother looks at Wayne and says, "So are you just going to stay here while we are gone?" Wayne closes his eyes and puts his head up under the cover as his mother says, "God sees you laying in the bed." Then she walks out the door.

It is now 10:30 a.m.; Mrs. Fuller, David and Renee are in the car on their way to church. They're greeted by other

2

family and church members as they arrive. Some of the older ladies marvel at how the children continue to grow and look so well. Mrs. Reynolds asks, "Where is that other fine son of yours, Wayne?" Mrs. Fuller just shrugs her shoulders and says, "I just cannot get that boy in church." Mrs. Reynolds says, "Well, at least you got David here," as she turns to David and questions, "David, are you here to praise His name? Are you here because He woke you up this morning? Are you here because you believe the Lord will never leave you nor forsake you? Are you here because you believe that through Christ all things all possible?" David says, "Yes, Mrs. Reynolds, I'm here because of all of that." Then Renee says, "Yeah, all of that just happens to be Tiffany who's singing up in the choir today." "Well, at least he is here," Mrs. Reynolds sighs.

As they walk into the sanctuary, David tells his mother that he will be sitting over to the left with his "homies." Mrs. Fuller would prefer that David sit with the family, but she lets him sit with his friends anyway. Renee is upset that she has to sit with her mother, while David can sit wherever he wants and Wayne doesn't have to come to church at all. Mrs. Fuller quickly tells Renee that she doesn't want to hear anything else out of her. The worship service was spirit-filled; there were praise songs and opening hymns, a powerful prayer at altar call, and the preacher spoke about an African brother named Nimrod, a mighty warrior in battle. Four people walked the aisle that Sunday morning and gave their lives to Christ. Mrs. Fuller was hoping that David would have been one of them, but she knew that in God's time that would happen.

Sometime during the service, Mrs. Fuller looked over at David and knew that whenever there was a Scripture reference David would simply have to listen because he had forgotten to bring his Bible. She also noticed that through much of the sermon, David was asleep. Had she been sitting next to him, she would have been able to keep him awake by putting her elbow into his rib, giving him a mint or doing whatever she could do to keep her son awake. She thanked God that he didn't snore like his brother Wayne. Sometimes she gave him very strong eye contact when she heard him and a few of his male friends talking, and while it wasn't when the Pastor was preaching, it did seem rude and out of order in the sanctuary.

After service, David was talking to Tiffany; she was inquiring about her singing that morning. Before he could respond, Tiffany's parents told her that it was time for them to go home. David says he will call her that evening, but her father says that Tiffany is not to receive phone calls on school nights. The Fullers drive home, and when they open up the door, Wayne is sitting on the couch with a can of pop in his hands, watching the Cowboys vs. the 49ers on television.

***

It seems like everybody is looking for the Black male. Black women are looking for a good Black man to marry. Black children, especially Black boys, are looking for Black men to nurture them and give them a sense of direction. Schools are looking for dedicated and consistent African American men to volunteer for role model and rites of passage programs. While many employers have very little interest in people of color, and those who do realize that they could hire a Black woman to satisfy both race and gender quotas, there are some companies such as my own that are looking for African American men who are skilled, articulate, and dependable. The Black church is also looking for African American men.

The following are two short stories from an African American woman and an African American pastor, both looking for Adam-the original Black man:

Jackie was everything that a Black man could possibly want in a Black woman. She was the pride of her parents' eyes, and she was very pleased with herself. Jackie had begun to worry; she had played it by her parents' rules, having gone to elementary school, high school,

4

and college, graduating with a 3.5 GPA. She even listened to her parents and went straight to graduate school, rather than going to work in corporate America. She secured her MBA (Master's in Business Administration) at the age of twenty-four. But now, at thirty-four, she still hadn't found a man. She had read Jawanza Kunjufu's book, *The Power, Passion, and Pain of Black Love,* and Larry Davis' book, *Black and Single;* she had even tried to implement many of the strategies of these two authors. She tried to convince brothers that they didn't need to have the same educational background that she did nor did they have to make as much money as she did, but for some reason, the brothers just did not want to hear that. All they saw was a sister who had B.A and M.B.A behind her name to go along with her $50,000 salary. She was considered fine by most brothers, but some brothers were intimidated because they felt that a sister who looked as good as Jackie would be arrogant and conceited. So Jackie tried very hard to be as down-to-earth as possible, the type of person that a guy would want to talk to--a real sincere friend. Her last boyfriend had broken up with her because he was irritated by all the stares she got from other guys; he also questioned Jackie about what she saw in him and why she wanted to be with him.

She was crying as she told her pastor that her biological clock was running out and that she didn't want to adopt because she wanted a child of her own. She also didn't want to be a single parent; she wanted a husband to go along with her baby. Was that too much to ask? Lord, is that too much to ask? Not having sex before marriage was difficult sometimes when the intensity and passion and romance were so deep, but she always carried God's Word in her heart, which strengthened her. "I never would forget when one brother told me, 'well, if you won't give it up, then someone else will,'" Jackie said. "I hollered back, 'Then go get it!' The sad thing is, he was right, somebody else did 'give it up.' I'm not asking for much, just a BMW - a Black Man who's Working. Is it too much to want a BME - a Black Man who's Educated, or a BMC - a Black Man who's Conscious? Is it too much to want a BMF - a Black Man who's Faithful? Lord, you tell me, is it too much to ask for a BMS - a Black Man who's Saved?" The Pastor continued to listen, as he has done in so many other similar situations. There is very little he could say, because he knew that all of her requests were legitimate. Why shouldn't all Black women have the opportunity to marry? Why shouldn't Black women who love the Lord have the opportunity to marry someone who also loves the Lord? Why shouldn't every Black woman who wants to have children have the opportunity within the context of being accepted by God? The Pastor knew that it wasn't too much for a Black woman to ask for a Black man who knew Jesus and who was going to raise his household on Joshua 24:15, "But if serving the Lord seems undesirable to you, then choose for yourselves this day whom you will serve, whether the gods your forefathers served beyond the River, or the gods of the Amorites, in whose land you are living. But as for me and my household, we will serve the Lord." The Pastor could only tell Jackie that she must "wait on the Lord and be of good courage." She was on God's timetable, not her own. The Lord reminds us that our thoughts are not His thoughts and His ways are not our ways, and that God's foolishness is much greater than all our wisdom. Paul said, "I would rather you be single for there is so much more that you could do for the Lord in that state." The Pastor shared with Jackie success stories of women who had sat in that same chair crying about the lack of a BMS. Many of those women who couldn't see it at age 28, 30, 32, 34, or 36 have now found their man. The Pastor pondered whether he should also share the stories of all those sisters who are still looking, seemingly without hope of ever finding that person.

Jackie looked at the Pastor and said, "You know, Pastor, yesterday in the service, I looked on my pew and there were fifteen people; all of them were women. Now tell me, what are my chances of finding a BMS? "I have so many girlfriends who tell me that they thought they were going to change their man; they knew he wasn't saved, but at least he was a BMW. They thought that after being with them that he would eventually give his life to Christ. In so many cases, it has not happened. I know the church is where I need to find him, but he is not here and I am running out of time. What should I do?" There is a long silence as the Pastor wonders if he should say that "weeping may endure for a night, but joy comes in the morning," or "right now, we are experiencing a Friday evening but there will be a Sunday morning rising." The session concludes with prayer.

One night as Jackie is laying on her pillow and the tears gently begin to flow, she prays, "I was looking for a BMW, but all I have is you. I was looking for a BME, but all I have is you. I was looking for a BMC, but all I have is you. I was looking for a BMF and a BMS, but again, all I have is you. I know that your grace is sufficient." Then she thinks to herself, "I was looking for Adam, I was looking for the Black man, and now I'm going to steal away with Jesus." She smiles as she goes to bed wondering if she could take Jesus as her date to the United Negro College Fund Banquet next Saturday, wondering if Jesus could go with her on vacation next month to Aruba and meet her in Quincy Jones's garden.

***

It is Monday morning and Reverend Washington is driving to his church, First Baptist. The congregation has 300 members, and yesterday was Men's Day. His sermon title was "Where Are the Men?" It is ironic that as he drives down the avenue to his church on this particular day, he sees several brothers just hanging out on the corner near liquor stores, at the tire shop, sitting on garbage cans - as if God is answering his question from the previous Sunday morning's sermon. Reverend Washington ponders whether or not he was asking a rhetorical question on that Sunday morning or asking a question that he did not know the answer to. Had he not seen these brothers last week, or on Saturday night, or even on Sunday morning, while on his way to First Baptist? Was he asking this question to the wrong group of members? Should he have stopped his car and asked them whether they were going to church, or why were they not going? With First Baptist having a population of 300, of which 75 percent were female, was it appropriate to ask 225 sisters where the brothers were? Did it make him look more appealing to those sisters when he raised that question? Did he expect the sisters to be able to answer that question? Did he even know the answer? He reflected on the loud response he got from the sisters during his sermon entitled, "Where Are You Adam? Where Are You Black Man? I Want to Have a Talk with You." Did Reverend Washington really want to have a talk with Adam? Why was he raising the Adam question in a congregation of 225 Eves? After service yesterday, Deacon Stewart said he thought the sermon was powerful, but he was offended that when Reverend Washington talked about the state of Black men, he was only describing those Black men that were out of the church. Reverend Washington's sermon had very little to offer Deacon Stewart and other brothers like him that were trying to do God's will, trying to do the right thing, by being in church. Reverend Washington was still wrestling with Deacon Stewart's major question, "Why do so many pastors browbeat the few men that are in the church? Is there any good news for the brothers that are in the church trying to do God's will, trying to help the pastor?"

Many of us have heard that the people who need to be here aren't here; the message or sermon is being delivered to the choir. Reverend Washington has been asked on numerous occasions by the sisters, "Where are the

Men?" He wants to develop a new ministry program for the brothers that he just drove by, because he realizes that yesterday's Men's week sermon had nothing to do with the people whom he saw as he drove into First Baptist. We still have 225 women and 75 men. He saw more than 75 brothers standing out along the avenue on his way to church. On this day he promises the Lord and himself that his ministry has got to speak to the brothers outside of the church.

CHAPTER 2

The State of the Black Church

I become very concerned when listening to conversations and absolute and extreme words are used, such as always, never, and only. These words exaggerate the conditions and make discussions monolithic. Friends and associates tell me that all Black churches are the same and that there is not one progressive church in their city. This chapter is an attempt to describe the diversity in the African American Church. There are numerous variables to consider and postulate as we try to better understand the African American Church. The epic study by C. Eric Lincoln and Lawrence Mamiya, *The Black Church in the African American Experience,* was an exhaustive survey of the ministries at 2,150 churches. As comprehensive as the survey is, it does not even scratch the surface toward fully understanding the over 75,000 African American churches nationwide.

The factors that Lincoln and Mamiya considered were the denominations of the churches, whether they were urban or rural, the size of the congregation, the annual budget of the church, the number of paid employees, the priorities and ministries of the pastor, the demographics of the congregation (including gender, age, income, and educational attainment), and the demographics of the church leadership based on gender and educational background. When these variables are considered, hopefully everyone should agree that the Black church cannot be spoken of in monolithic terms. Let's look at a few of these variables in detail. In the study done by Lincoln and Mamiya of 2,150

African American churches, they surveyed the size of the Black Church based on membership:

Size of Black Churches		
Membership Size	Number of Churches	Percentages
1-99	564	26.2
100-199	381	17.7
200-599	576	26.8
600+	349	16.3
No response	280	13.0

Source: Lincoln and Mamiya,
Table 14, p. 143.

From the 75,000 African American churches nationwide, there have developed over the years about a hundred megachurches, primarily in large urban areas. The boroughs of Brooklyn and Harlem in New York, where Black population exceeds the population of some cities, possess at least 10 churches with memberships that exceed 5,000. These would include Concord Baptist Church, Abyssinia Baptist Church, Canaan Baptist Church of Christ, Allen African Methodist Episcopal Church and St. Paul Baptist Church. In other major cities across the United States, there are at least two to five churches in each city where congregations exceed 5,000 members. At the same time, in cities such as New York, Chicago, or Detroit, on the very same block where there is a church with over 5,000 members, there will also be a storefront church with less than 100 members. Further, almost half of African American churches are located primarily in the rural south and have less than 200 members. Again, I raise the question, "Which Black church are you talking about - a church with 5,000 members in Brooklyn, a storefront church of 200 in Chicago, or a rural church in Tupelo, Mississippi, with less than 100 members?"

The next variable that I would like to consider is how

the wide range of denominations reflect the African American experience. There are seven major historical Black denominations: African Methodist Episcopal (AME), African Methodist Episcopal Zion (AMEZ), Christian Methodist Episcopal (CME), National Baptist Convention (NBC), National Baptist Convention of America (NBCA), Progressive National Baptist Convention (PNBC), and Church of God in Christ (COGIC). Approximately 80 percent of all Black Christians are in these seven denominations. Because the Black Church is not monolithic, even 80 percent does not describe the entire spectrum of African Americans attending church. The remaining 20 percent would include African Americans who are Presbyterian, Lutheran, Episcopalian, Catholic, United Church of Christ and numerous independents. In Chicago alone, the three largest Black churches are Apostolic Church of God, Christ Universal Temple (Independent) and Trinity United Church of Christ. The three largest Black churches in Chicago are not part of the 80 percent reflecting the seven historically Black denominations.

Another distinguishing factor of the Black Church is annual church income. In the excellent book by Dr. Walter Malone, *From Holy Power to Holy Profits*, Malone indicates that the Black Church receives annual contributions of nearly $2 billion. It has been estimated that when real estate holdings and other assets are considered, the institution is worth $50 billion.

Annual Church Income			
Income Categories	Total Number of Churches	Urban	Rural
$1–4,999	23 (10.8%)	110 (07.2%)	112 (19.7%)
$5,000–9,999	224 (10.4%)	116 (07.6%)	108 (17.4%)
$10,000–14,999	212 (09.9%)	136 (08.9%)	76 (12.3%)
$15,000–24,999	242 (11.3%)	162 (10.6%)	80 (12.9%)
$25,000–49,999	342 (15.8%)	270 (17.6%)	72 (11.7%)
$50,000 +	543 (25.3%)	513 (33.5%)	30 (04.8%)
No response	355 (16.5%)	224 (14.6%)	131 (21.2%)

Source: Lincoln and Mamiya,
The Black Church in the African American Experience.
Table 15, p. 144.

Here again we see that the Black Church is not monolithic: 11 percent of our churches have an annual income of less than $5,000, and 25 percent have an annual income of over $50,000. (The megachurches mentioned earlier have budgets that exceed $2 million per year, budgets that place them in the *Black Enterprise* Magazine's top 100 businesses.)

Walter Malone raises very significant questions and provides insightful solutions on what the Black Church is doing with its annual income of over $2 billion. Does the Black church deposit its money in Black banks? Estimates suggest that as many as 90 percent of our Black churches deposit their monies in White banks. While every effort should be made by the Black Church to deposit its money in Black banks, in all fairness to the Black church, there are many churches - both in rural and urban areas - where a Black bank is nonexistent. There are also tragic stories of Black churches, Black people and Black businesses who have attempted to do business with Black banks but were denied loans. Blacks banks cannot have it both ways. If they want Black people, churches, institutions, and businesses to support them, then Black banks have to also be supportive with loans and other investment strategies to empower the African American community.

The current situation does not prohibit the Black Church from creating a credit union or a Black bank. I was pleasantly surprised when speaking in Grand Rapids, Michigan, to find a grassroots constituency had been planning, organizing, meeting and pooling their resources to raise the $350,000 required to open a Black bank in their city. Churches with sizable budgets could easily allocate the necessary resources to achieve these types of requirements.

Further, Malone makes the point that with the largest portion of the church's estimated $50 billion assets in real estate, a greater use of Black general and subcontractors is essential. A major criticism of the Black Church is that the only building development taking place in the African American community is the construction of larger edifices primarily used on Sundays. Second, before churches use White general contractors and subcontractors, they should be persistent (as Maynard Jackson was in Atlanta with the construction of the airport,) to use African American general and subcontractors. If a mayor can do that for a city, then surely a pastor can do that for his/her church.

Next in our attempt to distinguish the variability of the Black Church, we need to explore the demographics of church membership.

CHURCH MEMBERSHIP ON THE ROLLS

	Total	Urban	Rural
Average total	390	479	171
Average adult men	70	90	30
Average adult women	199	240	88
Average total youth	101	120	54
Average male youth	29	35	16
Average female youth	77	91	38

Source: Lincoln and Mamiya,
The Black Church in the African American Experience.
Table 13, p. 141.
Figures are estimated averages, sub-groups do not equal total.

For the male population, if we combine the 70 adult men with the 29 male youth, the 99 men now represents 25 percent of the total population of 390. The combined female population of 291 represents 75 percent of the population of 390, which means that the average Black church is made up of 75 percent females and 75 percent adults and elders. I sincerely believe that for the Black Church to grow, develop and thrive, it has to increase its percentage of males and youth.

External factors such as White supremacy, racism (both overt and institutional), unemployment, and other societal factors cannot explain the adult gender disparity of 129 or the youth of 48. White supremacy can't explain why Mrs. Fuller allowed Wayne and David to make the decision whether they wanted to go to church or not, while she mandated Renee's attendance. In my earlier book, *Countering the Conspiracy to Destroy Black Boys*, I mentioned that "some mothers raise their daughters and love their sons." They have a double standard regarding sons and daughters. They make their daughters come in early, and not their sons. They make their daughters study, and not their sons. They make their daughters do indoor chores, but not their sons. They require their daughters to attend church but not their sons. What is ironic and amazing is these same adult Black women are concerned about why the men are not in church. Well, the question I want to raise to them, "Is your son in church?" We cannot rationalize that answer with an appeal to racism. Wayne stayed at home because his mother allowed him to, David attended only because his girlfriend was there, and he was sleep during the worship service.

The ratio of female-to-male youth of 77 to 29 is a clear precursor for the future. When these females become older, having been raised in the church, and if they have internalized the scriptures, their probability of finding a husband who is a BMS is small. As adults, these 77 females will have 29 males to choose from, assuming the 29 males who were in church as youths will remain as adults and will avoid homicide, incarceration, drugs and unemployment.

The major purpose of this book is to understand the gender disparity in the Church. The 21 reasons that I have researched will be provided in chapter 5 and responses to these excuses in chapter 6.

In this chapter, I am trying to describe the demographics of the Black Church. The table does not indicate the age range of those 269 adults. What African American women tell me is that of the 70 adult men present, there are few African American men between the ages of 21-45, which is considered the ideal marital age range. Therefore, a larger percentage of the 70 men are over 45 years of age. Of the 70 adult males, the numbers between the ages of 21- 45 who are "available" and single are sparse. (There is a distinction to be made between being available and being single because there are some men who have made themselves available who are married; my definition of being available means you are single.)

I said in my book, *The Power, Passion and Pain of Black Love*, that Black leadership and the Black community must address the question of what we as a community are going to do with a ratio of three and four Black women to every one Black man. Until there is a consensus on sharing or polygamy, then we are still expecting one man with one woman, and that means large numbers of women are going to be single. Some women have said it is unrealistic to expect them to be without a man.

The next variable that I want us to look at within the context of the Black Church is the pastor's educational background.

CLERGY EDUCATION

Years of Schooling	Total	Urban	Rural
Grammar school (1-3)	.9 (00.5%)	4 (00.3%)	5 (01.4%)
Grammar school (4-6)	30 (01.6%)	19 (01.2%)	11 (03.0%)
Grammar school (7-8)	92 (04.9%)	63 (04.2%)	30 (08.1%)
High school (1-3)	166 (08.8%)	117 (07.7%)	49 (13.5%)
High school (4)	260 (13.7%)	206 (13.5%)	54 (15.0%)
College (1-3)	347 (18.3%)	295 (19.2%)	52 (14.4%)
College (4)	251 (13.2%)	201 (13.1%)	50 (13.8%)
College 5 plus	680 (35.9%)	581 (37.9%)	99 (27.3%)
No response	59 (03.1%)	45 (02.9%)	13 (03.5%)

Source: Lincoln and Mamiya,
The Black Church in the African American Experience.
Table 7, p. 131.

Although the survey did not ask about the completion of a master of divinity program or graduation from a theological seminary, it is estimated that only 10 percent-20 percent of the clergy nationwide have completed their professional education at an accredited divinity school or theological seminary. Despite an increasing number of pastors who are pursuing their college education as they take their ministry more seriously, in years past, it has been estimated that as many as 80 percent of African American pastors who had been *called* were not trained. For this reason I agreed to teach doctoral seminary course work because I am interested in encouraging and assisting African American ministers who want to pursue their education to the fullest. As my pastor, Jeremiah A. Wright, Jr. explains, "Preaching is the only profession where people simply hang out the shingle and start preaching." We would not allow that of doctors, dentists, lawyers, accountants, or teachers; but we do allow that of our ministers.

When I see three and four churches on the same block, I become concerned. I Often visit this place called the Black community as if I were from another planet and I do ethnographic research. My first thought is that these people are very religious. In the typical four corners of a neighborhood, there will be two churches, a liquor store, and either a ribs joint or a gas station. I would also conclude that these people would have to be among the most moral people in the country, with over 75,000 churches blanketing the African American community. Yet homicide is the leading killer of Black men, and crime is considered the major problem in the African American community.

I'm sure my pastoral friends would say that the problem would worsen if we did not have those 75,000 churches and that the Church should not be the sole burden bearer against crime, and I agree. I hope they feel the Church can do more to address our social problems. I think often about how those churches developed. Could church B be the result of deflection from church A? Was there an ego problem between the pastor and a minister where the associate minister was not allowed to preach as much as he/she wanted to and he/she decided to start his/her own church? Would the Black community be better served if we had one church of 800 rather than two churches of 400?

In the cities where I lecture, I often ask the client, "What are the five largest businesses in your city?" Many of them are hard-pressed to give answers. If I tease them and say, "You cannot include barber shops, beauty shops, barbecue shops and funeral homes," they invariably ask me, "Can I name churches?" I then ask them, "Well, how many people do they employ?" and "What type of product or service are they providing for the larger Black community?"

The African American community must critically consider that, if the largest institutions and buildings in its community are churches, what does that say about its vitality and diversity. I often raise a very harsh question to people: "Is the church the only thing that Black men can run?" Sometimes I become harsher and raise the question: "Is that the only thing that White men let Black men run?" Why is it that Black men don't run million-dollar businesses? Too much competition? How much competition do Black men encounter from White men to run their churches? How much competition do Black funeral directors have from White funeral directors in burying their dead?

How can a Church have a membership of 75 percent females and yet have females constitute only 5 percent of the church leadership? How can 75 percent of the Black church be silent in the church leadership? Can you imagine what would happen if the women in the pews became silent? Can you imagine what would happen if the women in the choir loft grew silent? Can you imagine what would happen if the women on the usher board and stewardship council were silent? Are African American men basking in power with no competition from White men and Black women? How can African American men rationalize what Paul said in I Corinthians and I Timothy and not read what Paul said in Romans 16 and Galatians 3:28? Have Black men found a niche of power in White America that White men don't want, and where they will not allow Black women to compete against them? Are other men outside and inside the church jealous of 75,000 Black men who run these churches, some without an education? Are African American male pastors doing the same thing to African American women that White people did to them?

People that love and fight for freedom should want to eradicate injustices wherever they see them, eradicating not only racism and classism, but sexism also. If you look at the seven historical Black denominations, most of them have decided that women cannot preach, nor be pastors or deacons. They can only be evangelists, teachers, and deaconesses. Jeremiah Wright says in a style that only he uses, "The men that seem to have the greatest problems with women in leadership positions in the church are also its biggest whores."

Pastoral Responsibility	Urban	Rank Order
1. Civic leadership	14 (00.9%)	Sixth (tie)
2. Teaching	358 (23.4%)	Second
3. Preaching	919 (60.0%)	First
4. Leading worship	22 (01.4%)	Fifth
5. Visitation and counseling	14 (00.9%)	Sixth (tie)
6. Fund-raising	3 (00.2%)	Seventh
7. Church administration	62 (04.0%)	Third
8. Leadership of groups within the church	38 (02.5%)	Fourth
9. No response	101 (06.7%)	N=1,531

Source: Lincoln and Mamiya,

The Black Church in the African American Experience.

Table 11, p. 136

It has been said that the legacy, strength and foundation of the Black church rests with the ability of the pastor to <u>preach</u>. A pastor who is an excellent administrator, teacher, exceptional counselor and civic leader is not valued as much as the charismatic preacher. I often ask people after church, "What did the pastor say?" Many of the responses are, "I don't know, but he was good, he was slamming, and he tore it up." The pastor did tear it up, he was slamming, he was on time and it was powerful. However, we need more than that. Pastors need to ask themselves how they would feel if an exit survey of their congregation produced this response. Many pastors have attempted to circumvent this situation by allocating a portion of the program allocated for notetaking or for illustrating their major points. Of course, that also requires that the pastor have one to four major points and outline his sermon. Many members of the congregation cannot be faulted for how they respond to the sermon because many pastors do not organize their sermons.

I'm very much aware of the power that the Holy Spirit brings to the preacher, thereby making notetaking somewhat difficult; however I still believe African American people would be advanced further if people could remember the sermon's content and if the sermon challenged them to do concrete things in the upcoming days. Would the African American community, and specifically African American men, be there in greater numbers if there was a teaching component to the ministry? Would African American men be there in greater numbers if more ministry time was allocated toward job training and entrepreneur assistance? Would Rev. Washington have been able to increase the number of men in his congregation if part of his responsibilities included civic leadership, talking to brothers on the street and developing programs specifically for them? Should pastors be faulted if they are evaluated by how effectively they preach and whoop rather than by how they teach and administrate? Author and pastor A.J. McKnight says that <u>Preaching does not change behavior</u>. Pastors are evaluated by 75 percent females and 25 percent males, males who may not even be in the 21-45-year old category. Do African American pastors know what evaluation criteria men outside the Church possess?

I have over the years described the Church in three categories--entertainment, containment and liberation. I define an entertainment as a church where there is a lot of whooping, hollering and singing, to the exclusion of teaching and working. It is a church that makes you feel good for the moment but does not address societal issues. The church administrators may have activities during the week, but they do not empower their congregation culturally, politically or economically. Containment churches are defined very similarly to entertainment churches except that they are open only from 11 a.m.-1 p.m. on Sundays and closed the remainder of the week. Of the 75,000 churches in America, how many would you estimate are entertainment and containment churches? I define the last church as the liberation church, the church in which Nat Turner, Harriet Tubman, Denmark Vesey, Sojourner Truth, Gabriel Prosser, Richard Allen, Ida B. Wells and Marcus Garvey were members. This church understands the liberation theology of Luke 4:18-19: "The Lord has appointed me to preach the Gospel to the poor and heal the brokenhearted." It is based on the liberation theology of Isaiah 58, where we must feed the hungry and clothe the naked; James 2:26, which helps us understand that the cross is both vertical and horizontal: without God's Spirit our labor is in vain, and work without faith is dead. What percentage of our 75,000 churches do you think are liberation churches? Interestingly enough, when I observe liberation churches, greater than 25 percent of their congregation are youth and greater than 25 percent is male. I believe that young, people and men respond better to liberation theology, and I will expand these thoughts in the chapter on Solutions.

In conclusion, it has often been said that 11 a.m. Sunday is the most segregated hour in America. Whereas the church in the early 1900s was the focal point for all activity, with eight out of every ten children in attendance, it is now a place where only four out of ten are in attendance, and of the four, only one is male. A minister once told me that she is no longer surprised when she hears outlandish and horrible details of violence taking place in our society. She says that if you are not saved, if you don't have a personal relationship with Jesus Christ, there is nothing you could do that would surprise her. This is the first generation of African American youth for whom God is not in the center of their lives. People without values, people without morals, people who are not saved are dangerous because they are unpredictable and without conscience. We still live in a world where we have all sinned and are inclined to sin again, but through God's word and the power of His spirit, we are taught the difference between right and wrong, good and evil. We live in a world where children have not been taught right from wrong; we have children growing up in families where they have not been taught that stealing is a crime. They have not been taught that sex and marriage go together. They have not been taught that life is a gift from God that no man has the right to take another's life. We have entertainment and containment churches that allow stores in their communities to sell drug paraphernalia and liquor to children. We have dope houses right next to the church. Liberation churches do not tolerate this type of disrespect; neither would Muslims. The next chapter will look at the impact Islam is having on Adam.

CHAPTER 3

The Influence of Islam

I was in the Deacon's car as he drove me to a church in Georgia where I was going to speak. Immediately, my feelings were hurt as I listened to him say that the Pastor and several Deacons were looking forward to my presentation that day, but were ambivalent about my Muslim faith. That shocked me because I had spoken with the Pastor earlier, and I wondered why he had invited me to speak at his church without determining whether I was a Christian who believed that Jesus Christ was Lord. I thought, what exactly did he think I was going to preach about? Was this simply supposed to be a Black history presentation? Was I going to talk about the plight of the Black male, the plight of the Black family or the academic achievement of African American children? Was he going to turn his church into an educational workshop? I would have been totally against these topics for a Sunday sermon at the 11 o'clock hour. The Deacon didn't notice my disappointment, but I told him, "I am a Christian, and I believe that Jesus Christ is the Son of God."

I went through the litany of questions that I now use to find out why people assume that I am a Muslim. Was it because my name is Jawanza Kunjufu? My name is not Muslim, it is African. My name in Kiswahili means "dependable" and "cheerful." Did he think that I was a Muslim because I requested bottled water and fruit, and no meat? Had he ever met a Christian who didn't eat pork? Did he think that I was a Muslim because I am Africentric and do not believe that Christopher Columbus discovered

25

America, that Abraham Lincoln freed the slaves and that Egypt is in the Middle East? Do you know Moses was an African (Exodus 2:19), that Paul was an African (Acts 21:38), and that Jesus Christ had "hair the texture of wool and feet the color of bronze?" (Daniel 7:9 and Revelation 1:14-15) Had he never met a Christian who was Afri-centric? I was dressed in a suit and a tie because I had decided that was one of the compromises that I would make as a result of living in America. If I had chosen to wear African dress, would that have also made him think that I was a Muslim? Had he ever seen a Christian in a dashiki? Is it not possible for Christians to understand economics? Had he ever met a Christian who owned a profitable business that employed people? Did he think that I was a Muslim because Louis Farrakhan, Na'im Akbar, Akbar Muhammad and I are friends and working partners? Did he think I was a Muslim because I am a supporter of the Nation of Islam's economic program and because we sell each others' products in our bookstores? Did he think I was a Muslim because Farrakhan and I mention one another in our speeches, or because Na'im Akbar and I are on the same speaking circuit, that he wrote the introduction for *Developing Positive Self-Images and Discipline in Black Children*, and that we reciprocally recommend one another when one of us is unavailable to give a speech? Did he think I was Muslim because I was invited to Ghana by Akbar Muhammad to be his guest and to speak? For all of these and other reasons, I now state in all of my books that I am a Christian, so everyone will know.

Of all of the things that I have accomplished thus far, one that is most significant has been the creation of a crime watch group, Community of Men. Started in March, 1992, it was born out of my frustration in watching news reports about murder after murder and my desire to make a difference. There were 175 men at our initial planning meetings. At these meetings we analyzed crime statistics; we probed for causes and we began to strategize about what to do to curtail crime. We decided that too many of our programs are structured without an outreach component. The consensus was that we should identify drug-infested neighborhoods and distribute literature to brothers and sisters about drugs and guns and their genocidal effect on our people. We wanted to entice them to come to a building we had secured, where we would mentor, tutor and teach entrepreneurship.

Several incidents happened in those first 120 days. We decided to be an organization where religion would not be the focal point; we wanted to be a concerned group of Black men trying to secure and protect our community, where brothers of all religious persuasions or no religious persuasion were invited. Jeremiah Wright teases me to this day that in the church at the first meeting I chaired there were Muslims in attendance, and they were trying to proselytize my youngest son. Clearly our agenda did not call for people to network and to push their own business, political or religious agendas. We only had one agenda-- to increase the peace. I expressed my discontent to the Muslims after that meeting; fortunately or unfortunately, they chose not to attend subsequent meetings.

When it came time to move from theory to practice, to move from the confines of talking about the problem to patrolling the streets, the initial 175 brothers had dwindled to 68 members. Presently we have 21 still on the battle-field for the Lord.

I never will forget when we first started; Black men wearing shirts and ties, walking through the community, standing on corners, passing out literature and mentoring brothers. People asked, "Are you Muslims?" After the fifth or sixth time, I asked them whether they were children or adults, " Why did you think we were Muslims? Why didn't you think we were Christians?" They had a myriad of answers. The children said, "Well, y'all were wearing suits and ties, and the only men we see walking through here wearing suits and ties are Muslims." The adults said, "Well, because you're walking the streets and Christians don't walk the streets. Because you're standing on the corners talking to brothers, and Christians don't stand on corners and talk to brothers. You're addressing the issues of crime and drugs in our community and Christians don't do that." So I asked, "Well, what do Christians do?" One adult said, "Well, they do a lot of praying, they build large churches and wait for us to attend, they expect us to turn the other cheek and not deal with the issue of self-defense."

As we dwindled from 175 to 68 to 21 over the past two years, I have often thought about the two different approaches of accountability: if a man was not there on a particular night and didn't call, we prayed for the brother and hoped that he would make it the following week. I knew that if he had been a member of a frat, the Masons, a gang, or the FOI (Fruit of Islam), that group would not only pray for the brother who did not attend a crime-watch patrol, at seven o'clock but was not in attendance, they would have made a visit to his house after their activities and made the brother accountable.

Three excellent sources on Islam's influençe in the African American community are a book by C. Eric Lincoln, *Black Muslims in America*; an article in *Christianity Today,* January 1994; and *Emerge* magazine, March 1994. Islam has now become the second-largest religion in the United States, surpassing Judaism with an estimated 4-6 million Americans. Muslims say they number six million, and even the conservatives knowledge that at least 4 million Muslims reside in the United States, with 45 percent being African Americans. There are many Islamic sects in America. The two largest are Orthodox Muslims (which includes fundamentalists such as the Shiites, Sunni Muslims and the group headed by Warith Deen Muhammad) and the Nation of Islam (which is led by Minister Louis Farrakhan).

This chapter is not an attempt to create a debate between Orthodox Muslim groups and the Nation of Islam, nor to create controversy between Warith Deen Muhammad and Louis Farrakhan. Neither does it attempt to describe the various components of Islam and the basic principles of the Qur'an. This chapter takes a cursory look at Islam and its impact on African American males.

What has made Islam attractive to an increasing number of African American males? An estimated 40 million people of African descent reside in this country, and only 4 out of 10, or 16 million, attend church. This means that 24 million African Americans could potentially become churchgoers. Further, if only 4 million of the estimated 20 million African American males that live in this country are Christians, those 16 million African American males could be converted. I also don't think it is accidental that the gender ratio in the Christian church is 75 percent female to 25 percent male, while it is exactly the opposite in Islam. With the age distribution being much younger in Islamic mosques than in most Christian churches, African Americans have to raise the questions: "What is the mosque doing that many churches are not to attract a greater percentage of men?" "What percentage of the Muslim minister's time is allocated for preaching, teaching, civic leadership and church administration?" From an economic perspective, what percentage of Muslims earn less than $20,000, in comparison to members of Christian churches in the same geographical area? The assumption is that Muslims seek out the low-wage-earners, while the Church waits for the middle-class community to tithe.

Let's examine the following two scenarios:

A brother named Raynard lives in a typical urban jungle in America. He has spent the last three to five years vacillating between the streets and prison. What

do you think the chances are that Raynard will be minis-
tered to by a Christian male in comparison to an African
American male Muslim? Let's take this a step further.
Raynard is in a church; he has walked the aisle and given
his life to Christ. Within the first 30 days in the church,
what type of interaction will he have with the church? Will
he become a member as soon as he walks the aisle? Will
there be one or two classes that he will attend if he's available? If he doesn't attend those classes, will there be any
consequences or follow-ups? Will this follow-up be male-
to-male or female-to-male? Is he expected to make this
"daily walk" by himself, except for maybe a once-a-week
or once-a-month phone call? Will he be expected or required to join an organization? Is there a mechanism in
place to make sure he adheres to whatever organization
he joins? (Remember the entertainment and containment
churches are normally not open during the week, so that
may not be possible.)

If Raynard had attended a mosque of the Nation of Islam and had expressed an interest in joining the Nation,
what type of follow-up do you think would be involved?
Muslims in leadership positions shared with me several
procedures. First, the Nation of Islam does not immediately assume that a brother who expresses an interest in
becoming a member of the Nation of Islam is capable of
his own volition of following the principles of Islam. The
brother is assigned a "Big Brother" who will be in touch
with him daily. There will be formal single gender classes
on how to be a Muslim, which would be on Monday,
Wednesday, and Friday evenings. In Muslim worship
services and educational experiences, men and women are
separated, because they believe many males lack the
discipline to acquire knowledge while in the presence of
women. Classes explain Islam not only historically and
scripturally but also in terms of day-to-day living. In
Islam a man is taught that his position in the household
is the head: he is taught to respect his wife and his

children; to be the provider, because all work is honorable; to respect his body as a temple and that pork, cigarettes, and alcohol are not to be consumed. He is also expected to give 10-20 hours per week to Nation activities, which could include doing work around the building, selling newspapers or being involved in special programs. Upon satisfactorily completing these activities, he becomes eligible for further learning and to become a member of the FOI, the Fruit of Islam, which is the Nation's security force. In the FOI, he is taught techniques of self-defense, including drill competitions against other mosques nationwide. He is taught the basic pillars of Islam, which are to submit to the will of Allah and to pray five times a day. He is taught the significance of fasting for physical, mental and spiritual reasons.

Minister Louis Farrakhan, on a recent *Donahue* show, was commenting to Phil about the 700,000 African American males in prison, at a cost of $18,000-$38,000 per person, with a recidivism rate of 85 percent. He described how effective, with minimal financial resources, the Nation has been with these brothers, as well as the number of brothers they have been able to deliver from hard drugs, alcohol and nicotine. I smile and feel pleased every time I see a Muslim brother coming up to my car, soliciting me to buy the *Final Call* newspaper, because I remember that just months before the brother was soliciting me for money to "cop" or trying to entice me to buy whatever hard drugs he was selling. I know that this turn-around is not to be attributed to the government, but rather to the Nation of Islam.

The basic components of the Nation of Islam faith are also part of Orthodox Islam, but with less Africentricity, with economic support being provided and greater attention being given to the basic principles of the Qur'an. I have had the opportunity through programs and speaking engagements to work with both groups extensively. Sometimes I become concerned when talking with rank and file members of the Nation of Islam, for many of them cannot have a substantive conversation beyond the initial dogmatic rhetoric. I become very concerned when it appears to me that many are following Louis Farrakhan more than they are following Allah and the principles of the Qur'an. In Orthodox Islam, I see more emphasis being placed on the Qur'an. In terms of nationalism, both economic and cultural, the Nation of Islam's newspaper, the *Final Call*, exceeds the circulation of the other Orthodox Muslim newsletters without any significant comparison. The number of schools is equal, but it appears likely that the Nation of Islam will exceed the Orthodox Muslims within the next 10 years. In terms of economic opportunity, whether it is the bakery, fish, power product or FOI security corporation, the NOI far exceeds any other Islamic economic endeavor.

The Nation of Islam includes a security division, primarily populated by members of the FOI. This has become a multimillion-dollar enterprise for the Nation, because cities around the country have chosen the Nation's security force over other private security agencies. These cities feel that the Nation of Islam security force is more effective, less expensive, and employs members from the community previously involved in some of the same criminal activities they are trying to prevent. Because these men have now found Islam, they understand their history and their culture, and they have been able to maintain safety in many neighborhoods without the use of weapons. I have even seen Christian churches use Muslim security forces to safeguard their buildings. That is almost as outlandish as Jewish organizations telling Black organizations who they should hire and who they should allow to attend their meetings. Both take place in the Black community because, as Bobby Wright said, "There are no contradictions in our community; Black people allow anyone and anything to enter." Can you imagine the Nation of Islam contracting with a group of Christian men to protect their facilities?

One of my observations about fraternity pledges, Mason rites, or gang initiations is the similarity to becoming a member of the FOI. A high level of discipline is expected, accountability is mandated, and there are consequences for noncompliance. I have often wondered how a man could pledge Omega Psi Phi in six to eight weeks, desire to be branded, and proudly say that he will be a Q until the day he dies. I have wondered and wrestled with what occurs in that six-to-eight week experience that makes him so committed to a fraternal institution.

I've noticed differences between Muslim and Christian inmates and how they're treated by other inmates. Muslim inmates are clearly recognizable by their disciplined lifestyles. A Muslim will pray five times a day, read The Qur'an daily, and abstain from eating pork and smoking cigarettes. Most of them will be knowledgeable about their history and will exercise in preparation for self-defense. They will also spend time with other Muslims, which to some may appear like another gang, but who inside prison are a group to be respected and left alone.

In contrast, many Christians are unrecognizable. They don't seem to stand for anything, and therefore they become the victims of everything. If the Christian male didn't pray or read his Bible outside of prison on a regular basis, why should he in prison? If the Christian will eat, smoke, and drink anything, why should he be respected? If the Christian is ahistorical, apolitical and acultural, what makes him any different from all the other inmates? If the Christian will participate in all the street and locker room discussions, which are derogatory, disrespectful, and filled with four-letter words describing African American women, then inmates will feel the Christian is one of them. If Christians do not value self-defense or bonding with other Christians for support, then they can be physically and sexually violated.

If Muslims form an Africentric study group, lift up the image of Malcolm X, and are visited by African

American male Muslims, they will be respected. If Christians don't study, portray Michelangelo's cousin on a cross and are only visited by White female Christians, then they will be disrespected. But if the Christian is unashamed of Jesus, prays and reads his Bible regularly, forms a Bible and Africentric study group, participates in self-defense training and can explain the African origin of Christianity and documents that Marcus Garvey, Nat Turner, Denmark Vesey and Richard Allen were Christians, he will be respected. If the Christians provide tutoring and legal assistance, they will be a valued asset. If the Christians will be unashamed of a Savior who looked like them and died for them, and bond together, they will not be physically or sexually violated. Frank Reid III, a brilliant pastor and writer, says brothers turn to other religions when they have not been exposed to the authentic Africentric gospel of Jesus Christ.

We must also make a distinction between indoctrination and relationship. A person can become indoctrinated in a very short period and superficially appear to be disciplined and committed to God. Whereas, developing a relationship with God, through Jesus Christ, is a lifelong process and may not always be expressed externally, but can be felt by a peace that transcends all understanding.

Over the past two decades, I've wondered if we are more committed to secular institutions than we are to Jesus and to the liberation struggle. The major difference I see between becoming a member of a fraternity and becoming a Christian is that the former requires work, and the latter only requires a confession. Jesus is a gentleman; He is always there when you need Him, but He will not come into your heart and your life if you do not ask Him. Jesus gives you free will, and therefore others blame the Lord for the violence and the atrocities in the world. God is not a dictator; His will is not forced upon us. Just as He gave Adam and Eve free will, the same applies to us. I wonder how many more people would be Christians if they had to earn their faith through the successful completion of study and work assignments in which failure would bring dire consequences, rather than receive it as a result of God's grace. I wonder how many of those 175 brothers would still be with us if we had visited them after our patrol and talked about levels of accountability. It is amazing how many educational institutions claim that African American males are undisciplined and kick them out of school, and these same supposedly undisciplined brothers are told by the gang leader, "I want everyone at this corner at 6 a.m. tomorrow." They all show up prepared to fulfill their assignments. Many males are contemplating which religion to follow. This chapter is an attempt to clarify some of those issues.

Without doubt, the Christian church needs a major public relations firm to portray its efficacy to the larger community. In my city, Chicago, in any given week there could be five to ten thousand people fed and thousands of people clothed by churches. Still, one seldom hears in this Christian country, "Look at what the Christians are doing!" The church's great success in these endeavors has simply been taken for granted. But if 10 Muslims do something constructive, the community says, "Look at what the Muslims are doing, and where are the Christians?" Yet when the Black Leadership Summit no longer had the NAACP as its host, and they had less than 24 hours to secure a facility, they did not go to a mosque to meet; they went to a church.

When Ben Chavis, former National Executive Director of the NAACP, founded his own organization to address the concerns of the liberal African American of the 1990s and beyond, he went to a church to announce the formation of the National African American Development Fund (NAADF). There was no PR firm to promote the role of the church in his endeavor. When politicians are looking for votes in the Black community, they go to the church. When we talk about "One Church, One Child," "One Church, One User," or "One Church, One Homeless," it is the Christian church that we are talking about. But the larger community doesn't understand that these programs are being orchestrated by Christians. Part of the problem, especially for those who only see Islam from the viewpoint of the Nation of Islam, is that they see all of its members following one person with the same programmatical thrust, so this sect of Islam has one leader, unlike the Christian church which under African Americans, has 75,000 leaders. Not one of them on his/her own, more his than hers, can fill Madison Square Garden with 25,000 people. The work of African American churches in Chicago or New York far exceeds the work of the Muslims. Consider that when Minister Farrakhan speaks there will be 25,000 in attendance, but when you visit the mosque in New York, or another city after Farrakhan speaks on the Sunday following, the number of people in attendance could fit in a small room. Compare the number of housing development units, day care facilities, and food pantries provided by churches to the Muslims' social projects and the Muslims projects are negligible. It's a misconception on the street that the Christians are not doing work in the community and that only the Muslims are involved in the neighborhood.

The next time a Muslim tells you to quit practicing that White religion and to follow the original religion of the Black man, ask that person the following questions: "When did Islam originate?" "When was the prophet Muhammad born?" "Were Muslims ever involved in slavery in Africa?" "When did it begin?" "When did Islamic slavery end in Africa?" "Did Islamic slavery precede Christian slavery?" "Did Islamic slavery in East Africa continue longer than Christian slavery in West Africa?" "Does it remain today in Morocco and Mauritania?"

I would encourage the readers to review the works of Dr. Yosef ben-Jochannan, such as *African Origins of Western Religions*, which points out that the major tenets of Judaism, Christianity, and Islam developed in Africa. Prophet Muhammad was not born until 572 A.D.. I would also recommend that you read the book entitled, *The Destruction of Black Civilization,* in which Chancellor Williams documents the Islamic slavery of East Africa, which preceded Christian slavery in West Africa. Although you would never learn of Islamic slavery when talking to Muslims, they had been involved in slavery. Slavery in East and North Africa began in 700 A.D., did not officially end until 1991, and racial atrocities continue to occur in Africa by Muslim Arabs against Black Africans. Many young brothers have been raised in the church by a mother who has managed to keep the family together with much prayer and Jesus. And these boys have seen their mother's strength, which they didn't see in their father, who walked away from the family and left them. They saw her perseverance; they saw their mama scrub floors so that they could go to college. It concerns me to see these sons leave the church and pray five times a day, without praying once to their mama's God.

I have two questions to ask these sons. Did Prophet Muhammad die for you? Did he say he was coming back for you? As we prepare ourselves for the next chapter, on the state of the African American male, I am reminded of this very humorous but real story that a gynecologist shared about a Muslim sister in labor for long hours. Finally, with much effort, and with a tremendous push at the point where Reverend Youngblood says the marrow meets the bone, where the heart hurts, she screamed at the top of her lungs, "Jesus!"

CHAPTER 4

From Boyhood to Manhood

Infant Mortality

At birth we lose more African American males than females. There are 1,965 deaths per 100,000 live births for Black boys versus 1,603 per 100,000 deaths for Black girls. Out of the starting blocks, the male shortage, begins with 362 fewer Black males. Medical research has not provided an explanation. Men erroneously assume that they are the stronger gender, but in all races females have a lower infant mortality rate than males. Consequently, Black women begin to experience the African American male shortage from the very outset.

***

Educational System

In America, tracking begins as early as the eighth day of kindergarten. Children enter kindergarten with a myriad of experiences: full-day private daycare, half-day HeadStart, or the experience of staying home and watching *Sesame Street*. Most educators are theoretically aware that girls mature faster than boys and have different learning styles. Most teachers have not altered their pedagogy for male students. Research shows that if a child fails a grade in grammar school, the odds are 70 percent that the child will not graduate from high school. Who would ever fathom that Jackie was crying in her pastor's office for a man that she lost when he failed kindergarten, because that failure left him with only a 30 percent chance of graduating from high school? Her man had already dropped out of school. What can an African American male do in a highly technological economy without a high school diploma?

As an educational consultant who gives workshops to teachers, I would visit classrooms after my presentations. I began to notice a decline in male motivation and academic achievement after third grade. I began to see more Black boys in the principal's office and a disproportionate number in special education and remedial classrooms.

Where are you Adam? Adam would say, he lost interest, after he left the primary division, which is where he received higher expectations, more nurturance, more hands-on activities, more group experiences, and a classroom decor that was more motivating to his spirit. He lost interest when he moved to the sterile environment of the intermediate and upper grades, where there were lower expectations, more ditto sheets, less individualized instruction, and less nurturance. He was no longer encouraged to ask questions. He lost interest in school. His parents thought he had lost interest in the tenth grade, but it started in fourth grade.

***

Special Education

I enjoy interpreting statistics and trends. I believe numbers can speak to you, if you work and use them properly. When I find that 17 percent of the children in public schools are African American and that 8.5 percent are African American males, then I expect to see the same percentages in every other category in our school systems, such as gifted and talented and special education. Any disparity alarms me into probing further. When I find 41 percent of the special ed children are African American, something is wrong. Upon further investigation, I discovered that 85 percent of African American children in special ed are male. What did public schools do with "bad" Black boys before special ed was created in 1964? Is special education designed to be a dumping ground for African American male children? What do schools expect African American children, especially boys, to do after several years of a diluted curriculum? Do African American male children placed in special ed return to the mainstream classroom on grade level? What does one do with a high school diploma based on special education classes?

***

Overemphasis on Athletics

Do African American males and females in high school and college utilize sports in the same manner? Is there a difference in the graduation rate of African American female and male athletes? Is there a difference in the graduation rate of those athletes, male or female, that are involved in non-money-making sports? What's the percentage of African American males that play in the NFL? Is there a disproportionate number of African American males playing in the NBA? How many Asian ballplayers are in the NBA? When was the last time the University of Nevada, Las Vegas, Texas at El Paso, the University of Louisville, or Memphis State graduated a Black ballplayer? What's the significance of propositions 14, 16, 42, and 48? Should we believe those African American coaches who say there should be less reliance on the test? Why did athletes such as David Robinson and the late Arthur Ashe disagree with them and advocate that Black athletes should not shy away from achievement tests? What happens to African American collegiate ballplayers who presumed they were going pro but did not make it? Where are they today, and what are they doing? What does the failed athlete do in a highly technological society when his only skill is running a draw play or dunking a basketball?

***

Drug Abuse

It has been said that drugs are the new form of slavery. The African American family is very resilient. It survived the dungeons, the middle passage and slavery. But this newest slavery, crack cocaine, has crippled the African American family. Why has the government created double standards for the possession of crack cocaine and cocaine? What is the chemical difference between cocaine and crack cocaine? Why does the former carry a mandatory sentence while the latter receives a slap on the wrist. Do you know another industry that pays one to five thousand dollars a day? What did the other four families mean in the film *Godfather I* when they said they would sell cocaine to the darkies; they're animals and have no souls? What is the relationship between gangs and drugs? Are gangs similar to Fortune 500 corporations that are simply protecting their market share? Why does America, with only 6 percent of the world's population, consume over 60 percent of the drugs? Is the problem of America primarily drugs, morality, self-esteem, self-discipline or values? Does America suffer from the dreaded disease of narcissism? What did Gil Scott Heron mean in his song, "Message to the Messenger," by saying "If it is drug-related, there is no need to investigate?" How many marriages have been destroyed by the addictions of African American men? How many African American males make crack their God? Why do some African American men choose crack over Christ?

***

Economics

Can an African American man be a man in this country without a job? Can an African American be a man in this country without money? If African American men are lazy, why were they brought to this country? Could America have become the richest country in the world without free African labor for 246 years? Did African American men only become lazy in 1994? Why were 90 percent of African American fathers at home in 1920, 80 percent in 1960, and only 38 percent in 1994? Was the loss of the African American father related to the move from an agricultural to an industrial to a computer economy? What is America going to do with people they no longer need? What is the African American response? How long should African American women stay with their men when they are unemployed? What should an African American man do when he is unemployed--abuse his wife, and children, drink and smoke more, read the Bible, pursue an education, become a househusband, sell newspapers or bean pies? What wage rate is acceptable when Mexico pays $2.38 per hour and South Korea pays 75 cents an hour?

***

Homicide/Suicide

Why do African American men kill African American men? Why do African American males kill men of their own race? Why is homicide second only to AIDS in killing African American males? Was Tupac acting in the movie *Juice*? In Baltimore, why is Little Italy safer than the ghetto? Will a metal detector remove self-hatred? If White people have more guns, why do they have a lower homicide rate? If an African American woman was walking down the street late at night by herself, would she feel more comfortable if the person walking toward her was

43

an African American man, an African American woman, a White man, or a White woman? Why don't African American men protect African American children and elders? How could African American males attack the queen of the Civil Rights movement Rosa Parks? What is the difference between Black homicide and Black suicide? If an African American male involved in a 90-mile-per-hour car chase with the police dies, was that an accident or suicide? If it's five Bloods against twenty Crips, and the five Bloods die, was that homicide or suicide? Why do most White males commit suicide when their future is behind them, while most African American males commit suicide when their future is ahead of them? If men are stronger than women, why is their suicide rate greater than that of women? If African American women are weak, why do they commit suicide less than others?

***

Prison

Why are there more brothers in prison than in college? Is prison cheaper? Is prison more effective? Why does America send more people to prison than any other country in the world except Russia? Did you know that 95 percent of the brothers in prison can't read beyond the sixth-grade reading level, never graduated from high school, were never given a course in African history, were on the corners throughout the night, and did not attend Sunday School? What can we learn from this? Why have criminologists dropped the word *rehabilitation*? Why was "monster," Cody Scott, freely allowed to teach brothers how to kill each other but was placed in solitary confinement when he became Sanyika Shakur and tried to teach brothers Africentricity and Black-on-Black love? Why did Nathan McCall receive thirty days for almost killing a Black male, but twelve years for robbing a White store with no injuries?

***

Life Expectancy

Black males leave early on the front page of life due to infant mortality, leave in their prime due to homicide and suicide, and prematurely on the back page of life due to medical neglect. Why do Black men pay Social Security when many won't live to collect it? When is someone going to propose to Congress that African Americans be allowed to receive benefits at an earlier age? Why do African American men live longer when they are married? When was the last time you had a medical examination? Is it more macho and masculine to ignore ailments and pain? Would it have been more beneficial to your family to have seen a doctor? What do African American women do in the golden years of their lives, between 65 and 75 years of age, without their men? Should we begin taking our trips around the world before sixty-five?

When I raise the question, Where are you Adam? When I ask why most African American men don't go to church, I am left wanting, searching, and grasping for additional answers. The educator, sociologist, and psychologist dwell on such factors as infant mortality, failing kindergarten, the fourth-grade syndrome, special education, mothers with double standards for their sons and daughters, the disproportionate number of African American males suspended or dropped out, the overemphasis on athletics over academics, and drug usage and distribution. They dwell on the disproportionate number of African American men in the military, primarily on the front lines. I read the leading national figures for homicide, suicide, unemployment, incarceration, and AIDS. The male shortage is further exacerbated when Black men become sexually involved with men or non-African women. The above factors, although very significant, do not satisfy my quest to find out where Adam is on Sunday morning.

To those brothers not dead, not in hospitals, not high, not

hanging out on corners, not in jail, and not in mental institutions, where are you Adam, at eleven o'clock on Sunday morning? I drove around the city after an eight o'clock worship service. I drove all over the city where African Americans lived. I wanted to find out what African American males were doing at eleven. It was a beautiful morning in early September, and while driving down the block, I saw what I guessed was a mother and two daughters leaving the house at about 10:40 a.m. They appeared to be going to church. The man of the house was cutting the grass; I watched him and wondered why he preferred staying home. This brother, who appeared to be the husband and the father of this family, lived in a middle-income neighborhood; the block was well-maintained, each lawn carefully manicured. It seemed he helped, if he did not totally provide for, a very acceptable standard of living. He was not part of the plethora of previously cited statistics. He seemed very concerned about his lawn; he carefully mowed row after row, each properly lined up next to the other. Any grass that did not make the grass catcher was raked. He weeded on his knees, put additional rocks around the flower bed, and then watered the grass. He took great pride in observing that there were no dandelions. This appeared to be the type of brother that every sister would want. He was a BMW, but he was not a BMS - not a Black man saved. I would have liked to talk with him, to find out if he had ever gone to church, and if so, why he left. What are the factors that prohibit or discourage his attendance? I would have liked to talk with his wife about how she feels going to church while he cuts the grass. There are so many women who are married whose husbands are not in church. Not only do we have women without men, we have women with husbands who are not in church who struggle and wrestle to keep harmonious homes.

I then drove by an automobile plant, where the shifts were 7 to 3, 3 to 11, and 11 to 7. I knew that this plant on the outskirts of the city has a 40 percent African American male workforce. Over 500 cars in the parking lot on a Sunday morning meant that there were approximately 200 African American men in the plant on Sunday morning at eleven o'clock. This is a situation where the statistics do not inform us of Adam's whereabouts. These brothers could be committed to their wives, children and the Lord, but unfortunately have to work Sundays. We hear so much about African American men hanging out on corners and being involved in homicides and suicides. But how often do we hear about the large number of African Americans men that are improving the quality of their homes on Sunday morning or working to bring additional income into their homes? Sitting in my car thinking of where I would next observe, I started smiling, because so many African American women ask me, "Where can I find a man?" As I wrote in *The Power, Passion and Pain of Black Love,* there is a science to finding a mate; I should have invited those African American women to ride with me as I looked for Adam on Sunday morning.

The third place I chose to visit was the most popular basketball court in the city, which attracted a large number of brothers. I knew that the most competitive games were usually on Sunday mornings, ironically at eleven o'clock. The eighty or more brothers around the court waiting for their game to start were not just teeny-boppers, they were between the ages of 25 and 45, which is prime marital age range. I looked around the park and the court, but there was not one sister within 500 yards. Where are the brothers Sunday morning at eleven? They're playing basketball, working or improving their homes. These brothers were very intense. They were strategizing, staying in shape and monitoring their weight. These brothers were talking trash and signifying with each other with a great degree of camaraderie. The brothers seemed to go back a long way. I am sure that every pastor would have loved to have had these 80 brothers in their sanctuary this Sunday morning. Sadly, there were more brothers on this one basketball court than some churches had in their entire congregation. (If you recall, the average church has 390 members, 70 of whom are adult males.) How unfortunate that African American males have a greater commitment to a hoop than to the Holy Spirit, to a basketball than to a balm in Gilead, to a court than to Christ.

I decided to stay in the sports arena. Sports reminded me of playing jeopardy and for 20 points I predicted that brothers would also be on the golf course. I drove four miles to a popular course where African Americans have recently been admitted. As expected, 20 to 25 brothers were playing golf. These brothers were between 40 and 60 years of age, an ideal marital age range for a divorcee or a widow. Most of them had golf carts and wore better dress pants than some brothers wear to a party. There wasn't one African American woman on the entire golf course. Where are African American men Sunday morning at eleven? They are on the golf course playing eighteen holes; they may not return before 1:30 p.m. when their wives return home from church. I thought about what their wives or significant others were thinking while they were teeing off hole seven, the women in church praising God and their man praising his last putt. It was such a beautiful day: the grass was a deep green, the sky was a powder blue and the sun had a ray to it that reminded me of Amon Ra.

I chose to stay in the sports category for 40 points and moved to the bowling alley. Throughout the week there were competitive leagues, female, male and coed, but on Sunday morning at 11 a.m. the most competitive male league played. I went to the most popular bowling alley among African American males, with 30 teams of six bowlers each. The league had 180 African American males. While non-league bowling may be inexpensive, averaging between $1.50 and $2 per game, league bowling is more expensive because of the trophies and administrative expenses. Most bowlers spend $40 per week plus their betting money for high series, high game, strikes, and difficult spares. A brother could easily spend $20 on Sunday bowling, and many brothers are in several leagues. This does not include their obsessive practicing between leagues. A brother who spends $20 per week multiplied by four weeks is spending $80 per month. His annual expenses will be $1,060. A brother enrolled in three leagues will spend $3,180 in a year. I began to laugh, because many brothers complain about the money their wives give to the church, and yet they can find $1,060 for one league. As I continued to watch them enjoy themselves, I thought about what their wives might be thinking while in church: she was praising the Savior and he was praising a strike.

I wanted to play this sports category for sixty points, and chose to visit the softball diamonds. During the summer this is a very popular activity for African American males. At Shabazz Park, I saw twenty teams. I did see two women with the teams, cheering for the men and keeping the pop and beer cool while they played. Hopefully these sisters attended an earlier service, but maybe they, like the brothers, preferred being at the park on Sunday morning rather than in church. As I began to drive off, one man slid into second base, I wondered if he would work for the Lord with the same enthusiasm.

I thought of other sports that African American males could be involved in this Sunday morning. Later in the fall they would be involved in football. For one hundred points, I thought of tennis. I traveled to the "buppy" neighborhood tennis courts and found 16 brothers on eight courts and several brothers waiting. Like the golfers, they looked very affluent. Their cars were expensive, and they were enjoying themselves. I could determine from their performance that they had spent hours mastering their serve and backhand. They were trim, lean, mean, and

possessed the same intensity as the brothers on the basketball court. I smiled for a moment and thought maybe
African American women could learn from these athletic
brothers. Many Black women would have sat all day in
church, eaten a large meal after service, lain down to
take a nap after a piece of chocolate cake and ice cream,
and never exercised once. In rites of passage program,
we teach boys that manhood is based on the Pyramid.
You must be balanced spiritually, mentally and physically. It was apparent this Sunday morning that the brothers were working physically while the sisters were working spiritually. How unfortunate it is that many of us are
so unbalanced.

As it neared one o'clock, a football game was sched-
uled on television shortly and I thought about all the
brothers inside their houses with a beer, pretzels, and a
sandwich ready to watch the Bears play the Cowboys. I
knew that large numbers of men were also playing bid
whist, poker, spades and pinnacle. While there were
many brothers in the city who actually played outdoor
sports, I knew we had a larger number of couch potatoes
that were inside watching games, possibly remembering
their childhood and living their fantasies through their
heroes.

I visited a popular sports bar with a large-screen
television. Bobby's Lounge has a large crowd for Monday night football, but even on Sunday at one o'clock
this was a popular place for men. At least 14 to 15 brothers were already talking trash about the Bears and that
this is the year they're going to the Super Bowl. Many
brothers enjoy watching a game as a collective experience rather than alone. Bobby's place was where they
worshiped the Bears and the Dallas Cowboys, while
their wives and significant other friends were worshiping Jesus and His disciples. I wondered when it was time
to leave if they be able to share with their women how
much they enjoyed draw plays, blitzes and post patterns

as much as their wives would share with them their thoughts about Moses, David, Peter, Paul, Esther, Deborah, Ruth and Mary. What would a man say or feel when she said, "No one can do me like Jesus." I'm sure brothers felt the same in Bobby's Lounge. It was like being in church with fellow believers.

I left the lounge and drove around the city trying to think where else brothers could be this Sunday afternoon. I noticed a motel in the heart of the city. When I was younger, I had asked my father why there were motels in the city. I asked him that question because, when we took trips around the country, we always drove right off the highway and into a motel to spend the night. I wondered why there were so many motels in the city, because they were not near highways, and people were not traveling across the country. Why would anyone be tired driving down 47th Street the night before and leave the next morning to drive to 55th Street? I remember that the first time I asked my father that question, he sort of laughed and my mother giggled. I knew that this was going to be one of those ambiguous answers. They had to look at each other and determine exactly what they were going to say. I drove into the motel parking lot, and there must have been 35 to 40 cars in the lot. I began to wonder, was there a family reunion in town last night? Was there a wedding reception? I knew it could not have been a wedding reception, because this was a motel, not a hotel, but maybe these were the guests from the wedding reception and this was the place that they had all chosen to stay. Maybe there was a Black leadership summit conference and the participants had chosen to support a Black-owned motel in the inner city. I would have preferred to believe those things, but I knew last night was Saturday night and most of these 35 or 40 cars had been driven there either by men that had come here and had picked up a prostitute or by men who were married and had chosen this place on Sunday morning to fellowship with their girlfriend. Again, I wondered what was going through the mind of each man's wife as she was praising the Lord while he was at the Lover's Lane Motel on 47th Street praising another woman's loins. As I was sitting in the parking lot, I saw a few men and women walk down the ramps and walk up and down the staircases, securing ice and other paraphernalia. I chose to stay there and try to capture the experience. I had my Sunday newspaper and I decided that I was going to read and observe.

I thought about a good friend of mine who lives in another city and runs a Rites of Passage program on Sunday morning. He told me that the men chose Sunday morning to run the program. I asked him why they chose the Lord's day and asked whether that wouldn't conflict with the men and boys going to church. He said they had voted and the best time during the week to have their meeting was Sunday morning. These brothers did not reflect the social pathology pervasive in our community; they simply did not want to be in church on Sunday morning and preferred being involved in a Africentric program that teaches boys how to be men.

I began looking through the TV Guide and was glad I had taped most of the programs that came on while I was conducting this survey. I discovered years ago that the most substantive and informative programs of the week come on Sunday morning, while the frivolous lightweight talk shows and soap operas are on Monday through Friday. Karl Marx said religion is the opiate of the masses, but it does seem ironic that while people are hollering and shouting in church, the more rational logical scholars are at home watching, "Our Voices," "Lead Story," "Tony Brown's Journal," "The Gil Noble Show," "The Bill McCreary Report," "Face The Nation, and "Meet The Press."

I wondered whether after church a non-attending husband who chose to watch the documentaries could connect with his spirit-filled wife. She returned home wanting to share with him the powerful sermon, and he waited for her to come home to share the informative documentary on the state of White and Black America.

I began to drive out of the motel parking lot and wondered whether there were other places and activities that African American men might have been involved in this Sunday morning while their wives or significant others were at church. It dawned on me that many men had partied on Saturday night. I will never forget a sister who told me that a brother had hit on her at a party and asked her as early as one o'clock where they could have breakfast, and she had looked at him and said, "It's only one o'clock; why in the world are you asking where we should have breakfast at six o'clock!" I realized then that many brothers at 11 a.m. on Sunday were asleep. Their wives had risen early, quietly got out of bed, showered, dressed, and tried not to wake their husbands. I drove into my driveway, spotted my next-door neighbor, and asked him how he was doing. He said things were okay, his wife was in church, and he had been reading the Bible, the Qur'an, and the Husia, trying to do a comparative study to seek universal truth. He said he didn't need organized religion, that he was benefiting from his religious studies, and he invited me over to explore the inconsistencies and similarities between the Bible, the Qur'an, and the Husia.

It is now time to leave my brief excursion into the African American community on Sunday morning and from a quantitative perspective to delineate the reasons why most African American men don't attend church.

CHAPTER 5

Why Some Black Men Don't Go to Church

I returned to the church in 1980, after a six-year hiatus during which I thought that I could function without the Lord. Over the past two decades I've been asking brothers who were not attending church what their reasons were. I have read many articles that postulated many theories. But I wanted a more expanded and comprehensive study of why brothers don't go to church. I've asked brothers to complete the following questionnaire:

Name
Address
Age
Marital status/parental status
Number of parents in household
Parents' church status

Educational background
Did you attend Sunday school?
Were you baptized?
If so, why did you leave the church?
Have you ever been witnessed to, excluding the Jehovah's Witnesses?
Do you believe in God?
Do you believe in life after death?

My second objective was to bring some of these brothers together. We had an overnight retreat to discuss their questionnaires. What you will now read is a brief summary of what came from brothers sharing, as I've never witnessed before. There were over 75 brothers in the retreat. Twenty-one reasons were extrapolated and discussed. We agreed that the questionnaire and retreat discussion would be confidential. The names have been altered, but the major premises remain intact.

(1) HYPOCRISY

Many of the brothers said that there was too much contradiction between what was being said in church and what was being done in the community. Dale said that he had never been able to reconcile as a boy how the pastor of the church, who was married, was always over at the house "making out" with his mother. At that point there must have been 30 to 40 brothers who had stories to tell about inconsistencies. There were ministers having affairs, ministers abusive to their children, ministers who said, "Don't do as I do, but do as I say," ministers who lived extravagantly while their congregation was mired in squalor. Many brothers mentioned how they remembered when ministers were the biggest dogs on the block, and they just couldn't believe that they had changed overnight. They told how many brothers who had been unemployed or had not been successful in the corporate world had displayed a shingle, rented a storefront, announced they were a minister and now had a steady income and admiration from the community, primarily women. They said the hypocrisy was not just from the pulpit, but it existed throughout the church. Many shared stories about what they did with church folk on the weekends. One brother had the group in stitches describing his party brother who would leave the motel early Sunday morning in time to go to church.

(2) EGO/DICTATORIAL

Many brothers joined in on this one, with the favorite line, "The pastor said." Many brothers were very irritated about always being told what the pastor said about this and what the pastor said about that. And "If you could just be like the pastor," and "Real men do this, and their definition of a real man was the pastor. Many brothers went on to say how much of a problem it was when the pastor came over, that's when we use the good china and the best silver and we have the best meals that he didn't pay for, I did. And when he's not there, we use regular china and silver and we eat leftovers." Many of the men mentioned that they grew up in households where their father was not there, and they observed how the pastor, with all his economic resources, always needed to come to their house for dinner. Food was limited but the pastor ate seconds while the children ate very little. Many men said that as boys, they decided that as soon as they were grown, they were going to make sure no pastor would ever have that kind of input or that kind of clout in their home. Many men went on to say that "the pastor may be in charge of the church, but he is not in charge of this house. I pay the bills here, and what the pastor said does not count in this house." This became a very emotional discussion, but I also knew that there were some other issues that were related to it in terms of the male ego. One of the problems that many men shared indirectly about their egos was the desire to be in a leadership position. If you analyze the structure of the church, you see that positions are limited, and many times if a brother demonstrated leadership potential, he was viewed as a threat to the pastor. I have always said that the measure of a good leader is how strong his number 2, 3 and 4 person are, because weak leaders are not comfortable with strong people around them. Some brothers said they were former members of churches and either could not present their ideas to the pastor, or they were voted against, and there was no other way to be heard. "The pastor has the final word. He is the HNIC (Head Negro in Charge). The church is not administered in a democratic manner. I want some input; I don't believe all the power should belong to the pastor."

(3) FAITH-SUBMISSION-TRUST-FORGIVENESS-ANGRY AT GOD

The next factors were faith, submission, trust, forgiveness and anger. These reasons were more difficult for the men to express. I had asked the men earlier who was their closest male friend, and when was the last time they talked to that person, and does this friend know their most intimate secret. I believe some of the major reasons why Black women commit suicide less frequently than anyone else in America, is because they submit and believe in the Lord, they cry, and they share pain with a friend. The men wrestled with this; many of the men mentioned that their closest male friend was back in high school, on the football team, in the military or in a college fraternity, and they haven't seen each other in years. Almost 75 percent of the group had not been able to share their most intimate secret with their closest male friend. Then I asked them, "Can you share it with the Lord?" The same group that had been so vocal when we were talking about hypocrisy and ego had a very difficult time grappling with this one. "I stopped believing in God when He took my mother from me when I was only 10-years-old. No God would take someone's mama. How can I believe in a *Heavenly* father, when I don't know or believe in my *earthly* father?" One brother said, "I can't believe in anything that I can't see; I can't believe in anything that I can't understand. I function best when I am in control of the situation. I know what I can do, I know my strengths and weaknesses; I'm not sure about anybody else." It became more painful when they said they couldn't fathom the Lord forgiving them for their immoral behavior. It became obvious that they had not forgiven themselves and had projected their feelings on the Lord.

(4) PASSIVITY

Many of the brothers said, "I don't turn the other cheek, and I don't teach my sons to turn the other cheek." Can you imagine, with all the violence going on in our community, me telling my son to "suck it up?" I tell my son what my father and uncle told me: "If you don't fight, then you're getting two whippings, one from them and one from me." They said they didn't believe that nonsense of forgiving seven times 70 and walking away from an injustice. One brother said men are conquerors and protectors and are supposed to protect their turf. I asked the brothers if they had a weapon in their house, and 90 percent of the brothers said they did, and "that's another reason why I can't turn the other cheek. If somebody comes into my house I'm going to do more than pray with him, I'm going to prey on him."

(5) TITHING

The topic on tithing took about three hours, because almost every brother had something to say about the church taking money from people and about how the money is being disbursed. Their comments included: "How is it that the largest institution on the block is the church? How is it that the person driving the best car and having the best wardrobe is second only to the drug dealer is the pastor? Hell, I would be able to drive the finest car and wear the finest clothes too if everybody on the block gave me 10 percent of their income. I thought the Bible said "What you do to the least of these you also do unto me." If any man desires to be first, the same shall be last. It's obvious the pastor must not realize that because the pastor seems to have the first of everything." Several brothers said one of the main reasons their *significant other* split was because she wanted to give one-tenth of "their" money to the church. "I told her, I have a problem with you giving your money, but you definitely are not giving one-tenth of my money." Many brothers chimed in and said a woman should not be able to spend one-tenth of the man's money for something he did not support. They continued to complain, "Where is the money going?"

"How many people are they employing?" "What types of businesses are they creating?" "You look at most of these churches and at best they employ three people, the pastor, a secretary, and a part-time maintenance person." When I asked the brothers what they thought their wives should give, many of them had mixed answers. They really didn't know what the answer should be, but they seemed to feel that 10 percent was too much. I asked them, "should people give a dollar? Five dollars? Ten dollars? What's the relationship between a contribution to the church and a ticket to a baseball, basketball, or football game or a ticket to see Anita, Sade, or Luther?" They did not have a clear answer, but many said, "I will tithe when the church gives me a job."

(6) IRRELEVANCE

Recent studies indicate that the major problems in the African American community are crime, drugs, teen pregnancy, lack of recreational opportunities, unemployment, and single parenting. The criticism was that the church was not addressing those problems. It's only open on Sunday and all they do is holler and clap from 11 a.m to 1 p.m. How are you going to address the problems with that schedule and entertainment agenda? Many brothers said that the King James version of the Bible just doesn't provide solutions to problems of drugs, crime, teen pregnancy, unemployment, or recreational opportunities. Many brothers said they receive more satisfaction going to hear Farrakhan or Jackson or attending an African American conference or workshops that speak directly to the issues.

(7) EUROCENTRIC

The brothers discussed the issue of Eurocentrism for almost four hours. I eventually had to conclude the discussion, because everyone had something to say about the White, blonde, blue-eyed image of Jesus proudly displayed in the church sanctuary. One brother said, "I will go to church when that lying image comes down. I'm not worshiping no White man. I'm not worshiping anybody that does not look like me. I got a problem with these Easter Bunnies and these white eggs. I got a problem with these movies on television, where Moses, Cleopatra, Jesus and everybody else is White." "Now I don't know much about the Bible," one brother said, "but I know he had hair the texture of wool and feet the color of bronze." One brother said that when he mentioned that to his wife, she said "What difference does it make? We need to worship Him in spirit and in truth." The brother said, "I just looked at her and realized how deep the self-hatred is and the fact that the legacy of slavery remains." She didn't see the contradiction in keeping a White, blonde, blue-eyed image, while saying we need to worship Him in spirit and in truth. "All I'm saying is that if we are going to worship Him in spirit and in truth, then why don't we take the White, blond, blue-eyed image down." One brother said, "That's why I like Minister Farrakhan, because in the mosque you don't see those images. Islam is the original religion of the Black man."

(8) LENGTH OF SERVICE

The next reason was that service was too long. Every brother had a comment about this area. "I don't understand why a church service has to last three hours, I mean from 10:30 a.m. to 1:30 p.m., and then they want to fellowship and have something to eat. I don't know what takes three hours. You can make love or give birth in less than the time it takes them to have a worship service." "What I don't understand," said another brother, "is that there are some churches, for example the Catholic church, and they have mass in 45 minutes. There are some churches that have services one right after the other, and they do it in about an hour. So I don't understand why some churches

61

take three hours and others do it in forty-five minutes. How many songs do we need to hear? How many prayers do we need to give? How many times do we have to pass the basket begging for money? How many announcements do they have to make? They could put it in the bulletin and I can read it at home." A couple of brothers said, "And you always know when the pastor is lying when he says, 'I'm winding down.'" Every time I hear a pastor say he's winding down, I know I can add another thirty minutes. Don't let the pastor say, 'Can I get a few more minutes, because I always get outvoted.' I want to say, 'No, I'm ready to go now. But they know when they say, can I get a few more minutes,' that somebody always says, "Take your time Rev." I feel like hitting that person upside their head and say, 'Speak for yourself.' I feel that when they raise the question they should take it to the vote and if we say no, that means, "You need to end now. And if you say you're winding down then don't lie in the pulpit and continue for another hour." A lot of brothers nodded when those points were being made. One brother said, "But the problem I have is that after we've been there for three hours, and they're opening the doors of the church, which can take another 45 minutes, and then after they have asked you a million times, 'Do you want to confess Jesus Christ as Lord?' then they review the sermon in the benediction." I wish all the people that don't want to be saved, or who joined previously, or those that have done both could leave. They should design the service so that those that want to be saved or join should be the only people that remain. I wish they would place the time next to each component of the service so that if I only want to hear the sermon, I know what time to arrive. I don't want to hear all that singing and hollering and I'm not arriving an hour early just to get a seat.

(9) TOO EMOTIONAL

One brother said he never wanted to go to church after

he was seven years old when he was sitting in church and his grandmother, aunt, and another woman sitting next to him started hollering, and his aunt knocked him in the mouth as she got happy and began dancing down the aisle. "They embarrassed me as they stood up doing some kind of dance, offbeat, kicking their legs and swinging all around. Ushers had to come with paper towels and water. Maybe that's why we haven't moved any further, because the few times the pastor does have something progressive to say you can barely hear with all the hollering and shouting. That's why, one of the things I like about the Muslims is that they don't have all that singing and you don't see a lot of people shouting. I asked them one day about that and they said, "What we try to do is make sure everybody can hear, think, and act rational." Several brothers commented "That's why you have the church filled with so many women, because woman are emotional, and brothers are logical and rational." A few brothers went on to add, "Not only do you encounter hollering and shouting from the congregation, but then the preacher starts hollering, stomping and shouting. You notice how many times they have the same whooping and stepping. I heard some seminaries offer classes in whooping."

(10) SPORTS

One brother said, "I could probably squeeze church into my schedule if it wasn't on Sundays. That is the biggest sports day of the week. I would prefer Tuesday evening. That is a dead night for me, but not Sunday, especially during the football season, World Series or NBA playoffs, plus it conflicts with my bowling league." Brothers from Baltimore and St. Louis said the pastors were really worried that their cities were going to be selected by the NFL. I can only assume that since Charlotte was selected that may have a deleterious effect on male attendance in that city.

(11) ATTIRE/DRESS CODE

One brother said, "I just want to know, do you have to wear a suit in order to go to church?" Sometimes I don't have a suit because of finances, but primarily because my work doesn't require it. I remember once my woman said, "You need a suit for church," and that's what really turned me off about church, because when she said that, then I said, "I don't need church, because they should take me the way I am." I can go anywhere else without a suit or a sport jacket. Why do I have to have a suit or sport jacket to go to church? I asked my woman, "Where in the Bible, where did Jesus say that I can't come into his temple unless I'm dressed in my Sunday finest?" She could not find it in the Bible, but she said it's tradition, and I would embarrass her if I wore my regular clothes." Another brother said, "You don't really have to wear a suit in order to go, but those church folks are going to look at you, wonder who you are, why you're here, and make you feel uncomfortable."

(12) CLASSISM/UNEMPLOYMENT

The brothers discussed classism for almost two hours. Many brothers said, not only did they feel you needed a suit but you also needed money. Many brothers asked, "How can you go to church if you're unemployed? Everybody looks at you when they pass the basket. If you don't have anything to give then why should you be there? If you're unemployed you may not have the proper attire. The church is made up of middle-class hypocrites who feel better than everyone else. What can an unemployed person do for the church?" One brother said, "There are two things I know in this world. You cannot talk to a woman or attend church without money. Both the church and the woman are only interested in you if you have some money." I knew from talking with the brothers that 30 percent of the brothers sitting around the room were unemployed or underemployed. These men were sharing their honest feelings about being unemployed. Their words weren't a result of reading the latest book on the trials of the underclass.

(13) EDUCATION

A few brothers said, "I don't feel comfortable being in church because I can't read. How am I going to understand the Bible if I can't read? How am I going to sing the hymns if I can't read? How am I going to read the opening response if I can't read? Half the time I can't figure out what the pastor is saying with his doctorate. I can't follow him, and I don't want to ask people when I'm in church what is that word, and what is this word, and ask, what did the pastor mean when he used that word? They say that you have to have a sixth-grade education to read the newspaper. Well, you may need to have a high school diploma in order to be able to attend church. I have a GED, but I still probably read at the eighth-grade or ninth-grade level, so I have a twelfth-grade diploma but I don't read at a twelfth-grade level. My math is not at a twelfth grade level." One brother said, "But I bet you can figure out what one-tenth of your salary is." The brothers laughed and said, "Yeah my math has always been better than my reading."

(14) SEXUALITY AND DRUGS

The discussion on sexuality was almost as sensitive as the one on submitting to God. One brother said, "It's none of their business. I mean my lady knows I love her; we don't need to go down to the White man's court to get a license. I've been with her for five years. I've been with her longer than some brothers who got married in church

65

or who went down to the White man's court. The church doesn't need to know who I sleep with. A man has got to do what a man has got to do. If my woman is tired, if she is *out of commission*, if she doesn't want to do me the way that I want to be done, I should be able to go where I want, to be relieved and have my needs met. How can a pastor who I see doing the same thing that I'm doing, preach that I'm living in sin. I don't want to hear that."

Then they want to tell me that I can't drink, that I can't smoke, that I can't have a good time, that I can't play cards, and that's all the church does is tell me what I can't do. The Ten Commandments should be The Ten Cant's. I need a book that will tell me some of the things that I can do.

I shared with the brothers an excerpt of *60 Minutes* which stated, "The French have less incidence of heart disease because they have a glass of wine with every meal." Brothers then said, "Cheers." Brothers didn't want to let this alone. One brother said that he and his lady had been living together for seven or eight years, and neither one of them were in church, and he said that then she messed it up and got saved. She came home after a couple of months of being filled with the Holy Ghost and said, "The pastor said that we are living in sin." And I said, "You mean after eight good years, you're just figuring that out? After eight years of being together, you loving me, me loving you, and all these *saved* people arguing and breaking up, now you're going to tell me after two months of being in church, what that pimp you call a pastor said? I bet she had wished she had been quiet, because as a result of what her pastor said, she's now living by herself and I got me a new lady name Jean."

(15) HOMOSEXUALITY

Several of the brothers said that the church is made up of women, elders, children, and sissies. "You notice most of the brothers that play the organ or piano or sing in the choir, how they got their butt going up in the air. They love waving their open hand. No wonder they believe in turning the other cheek, they probably want to be kissed on it. They can't defend themselves." One brother joked and said, "I wonder how many fags are in the Nation of Islam?" One brother said, "That's why I let my girls go to church but not my boys. I want my boys to be like me. I want my boys to be strong. I want my boys to be macho. I don't want my boys crying. I don't want my boys trying to talk their way out of something. I don't want my boys ACDC. I want my boys to be straight. I don't want my sons being taught by a homosexual teacher or being propositioned by one."

16) SPIRITUALITY/WORSHIPING ALONE/UNIVERSALISM

Many of the brothers kept distinguishing between being spiritual and being religious. They said that people think that they don't believe. Several comments from the group were: "I believe in God. I don't necessarily know what to call Him. I don't know what happened two thousand years ago. I don't know if He really fed five thousand. I don't know if He turned water into wine. I don't know if He healed the sick. I don't know if He died on the cross and rose from the dead and He's coming back. I do believe in a higher force, but I don't feel a need to have to go to a church, to a building, to a male pastor, and pay my 10 percent admission of all my earnings to do right. I'm a good person, honest, responsible, giving, and I'm the block club president. Some brothers in church don't do anything on the block. I take children to Great America once a year. I'm involved in the street cleanup campaign. When people need something, they come to me. When I see the homeless, I try to help them, but I don't need a building for that. I believe in being spiritual, I just want to do the right thing. I want to live right, but I don't need structure nor do I need other people around me to believe in God."

Some brothers said they had a problem with the hierarchical elitist posture of religions. All religions postulate that they have *the* way, and if you don't believe their way, you're doomed. They just can't believe that if there are six billion people in the world, and at best there are two billion Christians, the remaining four billion people are going to hell. They said they're not going to be intimidated by some Negro pastor trying to scare them into being *saved*. They believe there are good ideas and principles in all religions, and they're going to continue studying all of them and reap all their benefits.

(17) HEAVEN

Heaven was another very sensitive area, because they were reluctant to talk about it. But it was on the questionnaire, and I wanted their dialogue. Finally, William said, "I got a problem with Heaven. The White man kick my butt everyday on the job, paying me barely enough to live on while he enjoys a nice house and I live in the projects. And I'm told the more I suffer in the projects, and the more I do without, the more I'm going to receive in Heaven. I got a problem with that. I got a problem with, I can sin all my life and like the brother who was hanging next to Jesus on the cross, and at the last moment, he believes and goes to Heaven. I hope that every White person that was involved in oppressing my ancestors, I hope they all are rotting in hell right now. I hope they weren't allowed to make some last-minute plea and go to Heaven. These churches and these pastors are agents for the White man to maintain the status quo. Why do African Americans always have to suffer and wait? I want my streets paved with gold now. I want the same things the White man has, I want my Mercedes, Lexus or Acura now. I want my mansion and 50 suits now. I want every type of appliance you can think of. I want everything

I can see. I can't talk about heaven. I can't talk about a place I can't see."

(18) EVANGELISM

One of the questions on the questionnaire was, "Have you ever been witnessed to?" I knew this would be sensitive, because there was only one brother in the group that had ever been witnessed to except by Jehovah's Witnesses. Many of the brothers said, "Have you noticed that when you're in the shopping malls and the Christians are witnessing to people, it's like they pick and choose who they want to witness to, and they have never witnessed to me. I remember one time when I was in a gang, I even went up to one and said, 'What about me, am I not worthy to hear about Jesus?' The brother and sister talked to me, but I could tell that it wasn't in their heart. The Muslims seem to specialize in witnessing to low-income brothers. I wonder what the Muslims see in us that the Christians don't. Did Jesus die only for the middle class?"

(19) LACK OF CHRISTIAN ROLE MODELS

Christian role models was a related issue that I knew was also going to be sensitive, because on the questionnaire very few brothers had anybody that was really close to them. Most just had either a father or a male who had lived in their household who was saved and went to church. On this issue, I chose to go around the room so that they could see for themselves, and it was amazing; not one of them had a male that had been in their home who was saved and went to church. One brother said, "It should be obvious why we're here. Can you be anything that you have not seen? Can you be a Black man if you have not seen a Black man? Can you be a saved Black man if you haven't seen a saved Black man? If you haven't

seen a Black man tithe, if you haven't seen a Black man
in your house pray, it's going to be difficult if not impos-
sible to emulate him."

(20) STREETS/PEER PRESSURE

I asked the brothers what they thought fellowship was.
I asked them if they thought passing the wine bottle around
on the streets could be defined as fellowship. I asked them
if "anteing" up the money to *cop* was that fellowship. I
asked them where they felt most comfortable, where they
could be themselves, where they were understood the most,
where they were accepted unconditionally. I asked them
whether their women did that for them. Where they work,
does their supervisor accept them? Does the church accept them? I knew the answer as I was raising the question. Then I asked, "Does your peer group, the brothers
that you spend time with on the streets, do they do that for
you?" Almost 95 percent said they did. That's where
they feel unconditional love, where they don't have to dress
in suits, they don't have to use big words, they don't have
to provide a résumé or business card, and they don't have
to have x amount of money to be part of a group. All they
have to do is to be there. One brother said, "Now that you
mention it, I feel like I have church every time I hang out
on the corner with my partners." One brother said, "We
even have devotions, libation and communion."

(21) PARENTAL DOUBLE STANDARDS
FORCED WHEN A CHILD

Some brothers said they appreciated their mothers giving them an option on attending church. One commented
that his mother made his sister go. I asked the brothers
if they saw any other double standards in their childhood.
They said their sisters spent more time in the house,
sometimes because they preferred it, but most of the time

it was because they had an earlier curfew. One brother said, "Ironically she was two years older." Other brothers said the girls did most of the indoor chores and they did more of the outdoor chores. Brothers said they preferred cutting the grass, raking leaves, shoveling snow, or emptying the garbage, because it wasn't as frequent as cooking, washing dishes, sweeping, mopping, or doing laundry.

I then asked the brothers how many of them were forced to go to church when they were children? One-third of the group raised their hands. One brother said, "I kept a vow to myself that as soon as I turned eighteen and became a man, I would never go back to church. I hated service. It was long, boring, for old folks, and very little applied to me as a young adult. My mama said if I didn't go to church, I couldn't play outside or watch television. I didn't have a choice because staying inside without anything to do was out of the question."

These were the 21 reasons I have been able to find why most African American men don't go to church. They have come from a combination of research, the questionnaire, formal interviews and now this weekend retreat. I wanted the reasons to be presented in the men's own words as much as possible, unadulterated, unaltered, and without the immediate desire to respond and be defensive with a rebuttal. Whether or not we agree with these reasons, this is how many brothers feel. The next chapter will give me an opportunity to respond with possible solutions. I would also like for Christians, before you read the next chapter, to look at these reasons and list next to them your own responses. To the unbelievers, did I miss any reasons and which reasons are yours?

CHAPTER SIX

Solutions

(1) HYPOCRISY

Hypocrisy is a very significant reason why many African American men do not attend church. The need for consistent role models is important for everyone, for children, adolescents, adults, and elders. It has often been said, "I would much rather see a sermon than hear a sermon." It becomes very difficult for people to be able to wrestle with what the pastor said and what he does. I want to make it perfectly clear that I am in no way rationalizing inconsistency, sin and the classic statement, "Don't do as I do, but do as I say." There are some questions and some challenges that I want to offer for those that have used this as their rationale for not going to church. First, if someone teaches you about right and wrong and you both theoretically agree, then that was the correct teaching. If the teacher is unable to adhere to his or her own instructions, why should that be a rationale for the student to also violate the rule? Or to use the teacher's inability to be consistent as their rationale not to participate? Can the pastor's or teacher's inconsistency be a convenient rationale for men to continue to do what they see the pastor doing? Can males look for dirt about a person, not because they're interested in helping that person to walk the straight line but because it allows them to continue to be inconsistent as well? I had the ideas for *The Power, Passion, and Pain of Black Love* ten years ago, but because I had been divorced I felt that I would not allow myself to release the book to the public until I had been married for 10 years. I regret that I was so affected by the public, because the ideas I presented in the book are very significant and they could have saved and aided many relationships. I succumbed to the public sentiment, "How can he tell me what to do if he can't do it himself?" I now realize that regardless of my marital status, those ideas can still be helpful to many people. There are some additional assumptions about hypocrisy that also need to be clarified. Some people think that the church is a museum for saints, when in reality, as Jeremiah Wright says, "It is a hospital for sinners." I mentioned in the chapter on Islam that the Christian church needs a public relations expert to inform the larger community about all the great things it's doing to empower people. It also needs a PR effort to let the larger community know that the only difference between the people inside the church and outside of it is that the people on the inside are sinners saved by grace, but both parties, in and out, are sinners. There are church members who have given the larger community the impression that they are pure, sanctified, and sinless, and that the people outside the church are the only sinners. These people are liars and the truth is not in them. In addition, the accent is also in the wrong place. Many people write Christ off because of hypocrisy within the church. They see the church and Christ as the same. There are numerous examples in the Bible where the church had one position and Christ had another. Peter wanted to take the problems of the larger community into his own hands. Jesus had another agenda. When 5,000 men and an unrecorded number of women and children needed something to eat, the church did not think it could feed them and was prepared to ignore their need. Christ had a different agenda and fed them with five loaves and two fish. It is unfortunate that people outside the church evaluate all churches and the Lord on the basis of what some people are doing in a particular church. The classic phrase that you don't throw away the baby with the bathwater is most appropriate. You don't throw Christ out if you have a problem with a particular member in a particular church. Pastor Jeremiah Wright tells the story of talking with a brother in the post office who is ranting and raving about them hypocrites in the church. Jeremiah counters and says, "Come on back, we have plenty of room for one more!"

(2) EGO/DICTATORIAL

One of the things I respect most about Jeremiah Wright Jr. is that there are over 70 ministries in his church. Many pastors would not allow that many ministries in their church, not because they didn't think they were needed, but because of their ego and their inability to chair all the meetings. If they can't be there, then those ministries cannot exist. I've also observed Pastor Wright when he is in attendance at those meetings. He takes unassuming positions in deference to the person administering that particular organization. Why, on the rare occasion when the pastor is present, should the pastor coordinate the meeting? It's been said there are certain pastors that have a style of leadership that attracts leaders. Secure people don't have problems attracting similar people to them. But insecure people with larger egos have major problems attracting leaders to their ministry. Not every pastor has the persona to attract strong African American men to them.

Many pastors tease the congregation and remind sisters, don't go home and tell your husband what the pastor said. I mentioned earlier that often women were going home making that statement to the extent that pastors are now trying to reprogram their female congregation. It becomes important that sisters also understand their role in this particular issue. African American women need to be sensitive and attuned to the male ego. I do not say they need to be violated, disrespected, and emotionally or physically abused. Just as certain pastors have the persona of attracting strong men to them, there are also certain women who have the ability to make their men feel important without in any way negating their role in the relationship. Unfortunately, some sisters may remember what the pastor said, but when provoked they spout a litany of pastor's statements into the face of their husband or significant other. One of the tremendous challenges in relationships is to avoid wounding each other. Unfortunately, most churches are structured dictatorially. If the pastor doesn't say it, if the pastor doesn't do it, neither does the congregation. If the pastor announced from the pulpit, "I want 200 African American men to meet me on a drug-infested corner because I want to clean up a particular neighborhood," in most churches it would be done. Unfortunately if anyone other than the pastor made the request most brothers would not be present. And most Black churches are designed like a dictatorship to fulfill the pastor's agenda. Many brothers have had great ideas and either were not heard or were rejected by the pastor. I would recommend that churches develop an executive council that reflects the demographics of the church and authorize this democratic board to review all new proposals.

(3) FAITH/SUBMISSION/TRUST/ FORGIVENESS/ANGER

It is difficult living in America as we near the 21st century, a world based on scholarship and scientific reasoning and analysis, to operate on faith. To believe something seemingly so foolish and so simple as that the Lord was born of a virgin, that He fed close to 20,000, including women and children, with five loaves and two fish, that He was able to heal the lame, restore sight to the blind, raise Lazarus from the dead, turn water into wine, walk on water, was nailed to a cross, buried, rose three days later and promised to come back for you, most would say is far-fetched. From a human perspective, I can understand how most people would require evidence. In 1 Corinthians, Paul attempts to explain this by saying that God's foolishness is greater than all of man's wisdom. This message was not designed for your intellect to comprehend. In the 38th chapter of Job, the Lord finally had enough of Job complaining about his circumstance and questioning Him for allowing it. Finally the Lord asked Job some very probing questions: "Where were you when I created the Heaven and the Earth? Where were you when I created the moon and the stars? Where were you when I created the planets? Where were you when I created the oceans? Do you have any idea of how the sun and moon operate? Do you understand how the world that I created works?"

There was a college conference on religion where many of the renowned scholars from around the world had come together to discuss whether God is and whether you can prove it. At the conclusion of this tremendous intellectual interchange lasting four to five hours, an elderly African American gentleman stood up to ask a question. You could see the irritation among the panelists and almost read their minds wondering how he could possibly formulate a question to ask them. The elderly gentleman, in a style which only he could demonstrate, was ever so slow and deliberate. He asked the question between bites on an apple, which appeared rude and annoying. When he had finished eating the apple he concluded his question. "I simply want to know, after this great intellectual dialogue lasting almost five hours, was the apple I just ate bitter or sweet?" There were six panelists and each of them had at least seven earned letters behind their name. They didn't have an answer to what appeared to be a very simple question. "Was the apple bitter or sweet?" Finally the man said, "Only when you taste Him for yourself. I'm the only one that knows whether the apple was bitter or sweet. I know what the Lord has done for me, and when you know that you know that you know, all the degrees and all the hours of discussion cannot negate the personal relationship that I have had over the years with Jesus."

Let me attempt to address this faith question this way. Do you attempt to eat with your nose? Do you attempt to hear with your eyes? Do you attempt to see with your tongue? Then why would you attempt to believe with your brain? To believe, as the Scriptures read, faith is the substance of things hoped for and the evidence of things unseen. To believe is not an intellectual pursuit. It is not something that you hear. It is not something that you taste. It is not something that you can prove. To believe is not channeled through your brain, eyes, nose, ears or tongue. It is to be done within the inner chambers of your heart and the sensory workings of the Holy Spirit within you.

Let's make this more personal. Suppose you or someone you love has a terminal disease, according to several doctors who examined you. Do you give up and accept that the disease is terminal and fatal, or do you believe a higher force will have the final word? If you have AIDS, do you agree with the medical profession that there is no cure? Or do you believe that there could be other possibilities?

One aspect I enjoyed as an athlete was what it does for character and what it does to increase faith. I definitely believe it would have to be faith that could convince a basketball team, when they are down 20 points in the fourth quarter against what appears to be a superior team, and believe that they can come back and win. To be losing 9-0 in a baseball game in the bottom of the ninth with two outs and their best pitcher pitching, and your weakest batter at the plate with a 0-2 count, would require faith to convince the batter and the remaining team that they can win. What I also like about sports is that the team with the best talent seldom wins. The team that plays best together, but more importantly has the greatest desire (their faith is stronger), wins the most championships. If brothers can believe in God the way they believe in their team, our problem would be solved. If brothers can believe in Jesus the way they believed in Jordan, this problem could be corrected.

(4) PASSIVITY

The image is that Jesus Christ was a wimp. That He was passive and believed in turning the other cheek. The image of Martin Luther King is that he also was a wimp. That he advocated nonviolence, that he allowed the water hoses and dogs to prey upon him and his followers. The image is that Malcolm X advocated violence and at the very least, self-defense as portrayed in the famous picture of him holding a gun looking out the window. If Jesus Christ and Martin Luther King, Jr. were wimps and weak, then why did oppressors choose to kill them? When King's philosophy of nonviolence is described by most people, they drop the key word, resistance. The key issue is resistance. What did Dr. King believe? What was he against? Dr. King believed in freedom, and that any injustice or impediment to freedom, locally, nationally or internationally, must be eradicated. King and Malcolm X had the same goal: freedom. Their desire was to see their people reach their full potential.

Dr. King felt that Memphis sanitation workers needed to be paid more, that bus patrons in Montgomery and throughout this country should be able to sit in the seat of their choice. Dr. King believed the Vietnam War was morally wrong. I believe to take these positions was a sign of strength. I never will forget during an episode of *Eyes on the Prize* describing the march in Selma, Alabama, Civil Rights Activist and former Mayor of Atlanta Andrew Young was asked if there was another option than nonviolence. And he said, "Yes, it was self-annihilation."

We had about 1,000 marchers and they had over 5,000 protesters heavily armed. This parallels the European invasion into Africa and slavery, where Europeans had more guns and ammunition. To postulate that 40 million African Americans can use violence against over 170 million White Americans, who have more artillery than we do, is suicidal.

Another illustration of the strength of Jesus and King is that you have two gangs who believe, like some brothers, in an eye for an eye and a tooth for a tooth. One gang was the "Bloods" and the other gang was the "Crips." One Blood is killed by the Crips, and therefore, one Crip will be killed by the Bloods. Unfortunately, in the new math, if one Blood is killed, then two Crips have to be killed. Regardless of whether it's two for one or one for one, if we have leadership that believes in an eye for an eye and a tooth for a tooth, a gang member or two for each death, we will end up with a blind, toothless, declining population. We need leaders who are strong enough to say it's time to increase the peace. It is not macho or masculine to be blind, toothless and a depleted group. I would not want to be a member of a group that will not exhaust the possibilities of peace. I wonder how many Presidents and Senators sent their sons to Vietnam?

In the excellent documentary by Malcolm Jamal Warner titled *Second Chance*, he created a scenario where a confrontation occurred between two brothers. It appeared that the next day in school, they were going to resolve it physically. The brother's friend, or more accurately, his associate, gave him a gun to resolve the matter. This young man had a bright future. He was being bullied by the gangs and he chose to take the gun. He used the gun and killed his adversary. The documentary showed that the boy with the bright future, after a two-minute interchange, was now in a back of a squad car, no longer preparing for college but now going to jail, and his adversary was dead. In two minutes we lost two African American males, and two

African American females will be without husbands and fathers for their children. They will ask, where are you Adam? And I will answer, we lost two in the last two minutes because they possessed a warped definition of manhood. Fortunately, in this documentary, they received a second chance. Malcolm rewinds the tape to that segment where the associate offers his friend a gun. This time the boy says no. The adversary "fronts" him off, embarrasses him verbally in front of his peers, and for two minutes he has to "suck it up" and acquiesce to his adversary. He then goes on with the rest of his life, a brilliant future ahead of him. Unfortunately, in life, most of us never receive a second chance. I wonder how many boys we have lost because they wanted to be macho for two minutes. I documented in *Hip-Hop Vs. Maat* that brothers gave 37 reasons why they would kill somebody, they included: brushing up against me, stepping on my shoe, looking at me the wrong way, saying hello to my lady, eating one of my french fries and messing up my hair. We need some strong men that will increase the peace. We need some strong men that will teach our boys conflict resolution. Many of our boys have never been taught any way to resolve conflict except through violence.

If Jesus Christ was a wimp, then how did he passively overturn the tables of the money changers in the sanctuary? In that particular passage of Scripture, He did not ask them to leave. He did not say, if you don't leave I'm going to tell my father on you. He overturned the tables; a very active effort. He did not use his disciples to help him out, like many males who think they're strong, but they have to hide behind 30 other gang members in order to deal with one brother. Jesus dealt with the money changer by himself in his sanctuary.

Nationwide churches are also portrayed as being weak, and yet they have security guards who are both uniformed and non-uniformed in their sanctuaries. I believe that if there are any criminal acts in the church, the guards are going to do more than pray with you; they're also going to prey on you. If the church is passive and weak and turns the other cheek, and we need to forgive 70 times seven, then why would the church hire armed security guards? I don't think that if somebody stole money from the offering, the church is going to simply forgive them. I'm very pleased that many churches are teaching martial arts and self-defense techniques to all members. Several churches have formed a crime-watch group. This group of Christian men patrols the streets in drug-infested neighborhoods and attempts to give young brothers a sense of direction and some alternatives to selling drugs. But unfortunately, these groups receive very little credit from the larger community. Seldom will you hear people say, "There goes the Christians patrolling the streets." You'll hear, "There goes the Muslims patrolling the streets."

(5) TITHING

I remember a brother once told me while doing a book display that he hoped for a larger female audience. I asked him why, and he responded, "Brothers have a tight fist with money. They believe the money is theirs. It's as if brothers think they're going to be able to take their money with them into eternity. But women have an open hand with money and freely give it, not only to make purchases but to support causes and their church." Before we delve into the economics of the church, I wonder if the same brothers who are critical about contributing to the church, financially support any organization in the larger community. The problem may not be tithing or the church but male selfishness. If we have a situation where the African American male is not contributing significantly to any organization, the problem is the African American male has not found one organization in the entire community that warrants his financial support.

I'd like to request my male readers to list who received contributions from them last year and the amount. Did you contribute this year to the United Negro College Fund, to the Black United Fund, to the National Association for the Advancement of Colored People, the Urban League, Operation Push, the Nation of Islam's Economic Program? Did you contribute to your Black college alma mater? Did you contribute to any local organization? Did you contribute to Africare? I've often noticed that we seem to do a better job managing Oprah Winfrey's, Michael Jordan's and Bill Cosby's money than we do our own. We seem to see more clearly where they should contribute theirs when the larger Black community could far exceed their contributions if we simply contributed our 10 percent. My first position is that before we look at the 10 percent donation that should go to the church, are you contributing any of your salary to any organization in the larger community? If not, then the problem is not with tithing and the church per se but with your lack of commitment to any organization.

Let's pursue in detail why the church needs financial support. We will remove the image of the pastor walking away with all the money by empowering the brothers who are outside of the church to become the church's board of directors. The first agenda item is identifying a facility to fellowship with one another. We want to reinforce one another and begin teaching morals, values and a higher standard of living. The response to the ministry has been favorable, and to continue it will need a building. Our initial desire was to achieve our objectives without raising funds. The reality of our present capitalistic structure necessitated renting or purchasing a building because no one gave us a facility. Our first budget expense was rent or a mortgage. The board of unbelievers will have to ask the congregation for contributions to pay for the building. The second expense will be utilities and maintenance. The next agenda item for the board will be identifying a head teacher, sometimes called a pastor.

This person may or may not be paid, depending on the progressiveness and size of the church. They want a church that will be open seven days a week and a community that will be actively involved. A church with relevant programs for men, women, elders and youth. They want to provide activities for youth as an alternative to potential gang and drug involvement. The board of unbelievers that doesn't want to tithe wants a liberation church. They want the pastor to preach, conduct funerals, weddings and baptisms. They also want the pastor to visit the sick and shut-in and counsel when needed. In addition, the pastor should be the chief administrator of the church. The board also wants the pastor and ministry staff to teach weekly Bible Study classes and Africentric history and culture classes. In addition, they want the pastor to be a community activist and attend political empowerment programs.

The board has two choices, they can either assign church members to preach, teach, conduct funerals, weddings, baptisms, administrate, teach, and attend meetings or in the spirit of Maat (reciprocity) they can pay the pastor a salary. It should be commensurate with what other professionals are paid to teach, motivate, counsel, and administrate. In addition, because the board of unbelievers wants a liberation church, by providing programs during the week for both children and adults, this will add additional expenses, e.g., receptionists, staff assistants, supplies, etc. Ideally speaking, we'd like to have a family life center that would offer basketball, music, dance, arts and crafts. This may require another building or an extension of some sort. It will also require additional funds from the unbelievers as well. The board wants to provide a food pantry for the larger community and to provide financial assistance for those in the community in need. They want to offer computer literacy and other job-training skills. The worship service requires musical instruments and hymnals. The board totals the expenses and presents an annual budget of $500,000. It is a myth that the bulk of the budget is going to the pastor to buy more and more Cadillacs. In order to build, operate, conduct, minister, and provide activities, financial resources will be required. Unlike institutions promoting a concert, movie, or game, this board of directors determines their costs, divides that by the number of people in attendance, and assesses a price for admission. The church, rather than charging everyone the same price, has chosen, because Jesus is a gentle person, to ask its members to contribute. If all voluntarily gave 10 percent of what they earned, it should be adequate to provide for church ministry.

I remember a very powerful speech the late evangelist Tom Skinner gave, where he said that in Jesus' days on earth, in serving the needy, 80 percent of the budget went to ministry and 20 percent of the monies raised went for administration. Unfortunately 2,000 years later, many people have become bureaucrats, and institutions now seem to fulfill their own objectives and not address the original premises of feeding the hungry and clothing the naked and taking care of the least of these. Today we have social service agencies, the government, entertainment, and containment churches, where 20 percent goes to ministry and 80 percent goes to what Tom Skinner calls "monster," previously called "administration." Agencies write grants for $100,000 to serve the needy, with $50,000 allocated to the executive director, $20,000 for the assistant director, $10,000 for the other administrative expenses, and the remaining $20,000 for the people the grant was written to benefit.

It becomes imperative that pastors disclose their budgets and accounting statements to their congregations. Many churches are not operating with sound fiscal management and audited statements. We need more honesty and trust. That can only be attained with open, honest talents the Lord gave you are the source of your income. If you understand that the contacts and net-working that the Lord provided for you are a major source of your income, it gives you a grateful attitude, and you no longer look at the 10 percent as something you lost; you feel thankful that you were allowed to keep the remaining 90 percent. Second, I believe we should pay ourselves next. Unfortunately many of us define savings and tithing as whatever remains after all purchases. I've operated on the reverse principle that 10 percent of whatever I receive will be my tithe, and the next 10 percent will be my savings, and now I'm able to spend the remaining 80 percent on discretionary purchases.

It appears that large numbers of women understand the principle of prosperity: with an open hand, the more you give, the more you get in return. In Luke 21 the Scripture talks about the poor widow who gave her two little copper coins, which was all she had, while the rich gave what they had to spare. Motivational speaker Les Brown told me once that he can look at a church and determine how many tapes he's going to sell. Those ministries that are involved in prosperity see an investment in self-help and other kinds of activities coming back to them double-and-triplefold, while there are some churches and members that have the attitude that they're from Missouri. You have to show me while holding closed fists. Brown said those closed-fist churches believe they're going to take their money with them to glory.

(6)   IRRELEVANCE

I would agree that those churches that are entertainment and containment, which are only open on Sunday, only shout and holler, are exclusively concerned about Heaven but don't teach people to enjoy life on Earth, that are more concerned about "monster" than "ministry," are irrelevant. The church is not monolithic. There are numerous liberation churches, and I believe there is a liberation church in every city. They have a liberation theology based on Luke 4:18-19, "The Lord has appointed me to preach the gospel to the poor." To heal the broken-hearted and to bring sight to the blind. They're based on Isaiah 58, where we are challenged to feed the hungry and clothe the naked. A church based on James 2:26, for as the body without spirit is dead, so faith without works is dead also.

These liberation churches have a historical track record that dates back to Nat Turner, Henry Highland Garnett, Gabriel Prosser and Denmark Vesey. The first three were ministers and Vesey was an active church leader who inspired members to revolt with the books of Zechariah and Joshua. The liberation church spearheaded the 265 slave revolts. Richard Allen felt African Americans should be able to worship the Lord in a respectful manner and not have to be second-class citizens in the house of the Lord. Richard Allen felt so strongly, he and others founded the Free African Society and the African Methodist Episcopal (AME) Church.

Liberation churches are cognizant of the major concerns affecting the African American community. Most national surveys document that the major problems are crime, unemployment, drugs, teen pregnancy, education, self-hatred, single parenting and health. Liberation churches are addressing these issues, and too many men want to make the church monolithic and do not acknowledge that there are some churches patrolling the streets and providing employment ministries, drug counseling, classes on teen sexuality, tutoring, test-taking skills and scholarships for college. They offer self-esteem and cultural programs to reduce and eliminate self-hatred and workshops on nutrition and provide free medical examinations.

I also believe that people genuinely concerned about the church don't make their comments on the outside. Instead, they join churches and begin to make their constructive criticisms on the inside. After my six-year hiatus with the church, I felt the need to return to the church, rather than staying on the outside and criticizing it for its shortcomings. I had a prime opportunity to be a member of a church and infuse my Africentric ideas, which included a rites of passage program, a monthly study group and a crime watch group. I'm rather suspicious of people who make criticisms about the church while remaining on the outside because it's obvious that is of no benefit to either party.

(7) EUROCENTRICITY

I hope that everyone, especially African American men, will read William Mosley's book, *What Color Was Jesus?* Walter McCray's book, *Black Presence in The Bible*, Cain Felder's books, *Stony the Road We Trod* and *Troubling Biblical Waters*, Yosef ben Jochannon's *African Origins of Western Religions*, and the *African Heritage Study Bible*. I'm confident that once read, discussed and digested properly, they would understand the relationship between Africentricity and Christocentricity. They would understand that it is a misconception that Christianity is a White religion, that its origins are in Europe, and that African people did not experience Christianity until they were brought to the Americas in the fifteenth and sixteenth centuries.

Further, if people do not read the books suggested above, if they simply read the eighth chapter of Acts, they will discover that an Ethiopian eunuch was reading the book Isaiah, representing Queen Candace at approximately 32 B.C. He was reading the Bible before 1619, and Ethiopia is in Africa, not in America. Many Christians are culturally and biblically illiterate, and when involved in a discussion with Muslims and other nonbelievers, they can't refute their premises. African American men need to know that Moses was an Egyptian African, as stated in Exodus 2:19. Paul was an African, as stated in Acts 21:38. Jesus was an African with hair the texture of wool and feet the color of bronze: Daniel 7:9 and Revelation 1:14- 15. He came from the line of David, who was Hamitic. Hamitic people are Black. He was born in Africa before the Suez Canal was built. The Garden of Eden story is an African story, with the Pishon River being the White Nile, while the Gihon River is the Blue Nile. African Americans need to know that the basic tenets of Christianity, e.g., monotheism, life after death, water used as a sign of purification, the Ten Commandments, the Trinity and the virgin birth, are African concepts. African people in 2800 B.C. believed in one God and associated God with the sun. The phrase Amon-Ra refers to their belief in one God. This precedes Akhenaton, who sometimes is given credit for monotheism in 1379 B.C. The building of pyramids, temples, tombs, and preparing bodies through mummification, show a respect for life after death. At the Temple of Karnak water was used as a sign of purification. The Ten Commandments that were continued by Moses are part of a larger code of ethics sometimes called the 142 negative confessions, the Declarations of innocence or Maat. The original Trinity was not the Father, Son and Holy Spirit, nor Joseph, Mary and Jesus, nor the Greek Osiris, Isis and Horus, nor the African Ausar, Aset and Heru, but in the beginning was the *word* and the *word* was with God and the *word* became flesh.

I remember that in the 1980s there was a movement in St. Louis by community advocates to persuade churches to remove their White images of Jesus Christ. The movement was semi-successful, but it is needed nationwide.

Many pastors have told me it's easier removing the image from the hand fans and books than from the cross and stained-glass windows. But if the church wants more African American men in attendance, and if they refuse to worship a White image that looks like Michelangelo's cousin, because Michelangelo was commissioned by Pope Julius II to paint him White in 1505, every effort should be made by the church to remove the image before they raise the question, "Where are the men?" If the church can't remove the image, then the self-hatred may be so deep that they cannot fathom that Jesus Christ looked like them. Ideally speaking, there should be no images of God in church. We should worship Him in spirit and truth. The second option would be to portray him the way He is described in the Bible rather than in Michelangelo's fantasy. African Americans need to know that God never placed a curse on Ham and that Noah placed a curse on his grandson Canaan.

(8) LENGTH OF SERVICE

I almost feel that the petty inconsistent complaint that many brothers give, that the services are too long, could be resolved in the People's Court. My first question would be, is the basketball, football, or baseball game that lasts three hours too long? What about the three-hour concert you heard last night with Anita, Sade, or Luther? Would your partying from 11 p.m. to 3 a.m. be considered too long? Your card party that went on most of the night into the wee hours of the morning, would that be considered too long? Would hanging out on the corners for over six hours be considered too long?

It is a double standard to say that the church service is too long while enjoying other activities that last longer. The excuse of the service being too long is just that, an excuse, because people do what they want to do, and if they enjoy something and value it, it doesn't matter how long it is.

My next response is for those brothers who are consistent in their arguments that they don't party longer or attend a concert longer than an hour. These men are consistent. They are concerned about time, not the nature of the activity. The good news is that there are masses that last forty-five minutes, and there are many church services that offer an hour-long worship service.

(9) EMOTIONAL

One of the reasons that has been given by African American men for not attending church is that the service becomes too emotional. Members begin to holler, stomp, and dance in the aisles and speak in strange tongues they can't understand. Some men believe the church is for women and people that are emotional, and what we need in today's society are people that are logical, rational, and scholarly and that don't allow their emotions to overcome them.

I decided one night to observe men who thought they were logical, rational and scholarly. I felt the best place to observe them would be what appears to be the last professional basketball game that Michael Jordan would play. To bring more significance to the event, his last game was also the last one to be played in the Chicago Stadium. Nationwide, stadiums have developed a sound meter to measure the applause and overall noise level in the building. Stadium administrators use the sound meter to excite the crowd to a frenzy. If you have never been in such an environment, the noise is deafening. Home court advantage is so significant that teams play an entire season just to secure home court advantage. These grown men with all of their skills and logic are greatly affected by the noise level. It was said in the '93-'94 season that the Bulls could not beat the New York Knicks without Michael Jordan. That was not true. In the playoff series, the Bulls beat New York three games in Chicago, but they were unable to beat the New York Knicks in Madison Square Garden in New York. The same thing also applies to the New York Knicks. They could beat Chicago in New York, but they could not beat Chicago in the Chicago Stadium with the noise.

The announcer is introducing Michael Jordan and the sound meter, which is measured from 1 to 10, goes off the loop because the sound meter is attempting to measure sound beyond the level 10. Eighty percent of the audience consists of males, who I'm sure would tell me they are very logical, rational, and scholarly.

On Sunday morning a woman testified in church that she had prayed for her wayward husband who had been using drugs for the past seven years. She did not want to leave him because she loved him, and she knew that Satan through drugs was the real enemy. She was testifying in church that her husband had given his life to Christ and was now drug free. Before she could finish the sentence, her hands went up in the air and joy exuded from her that began to permeate throughout the entire church. The organist got happy, followed by the choir, the deacon row began to rock and the congregation caught on fire. I wish we could have had a sound meter in church that morning because I was sure the sound was comparable to the sound I heard in the Chicago Stadium.

I have two questions to ask African American men about this scenario. First, is the criticism that it is not good to be emotional and holler, or is it acceptable if it involves sports? Second, which event had the greater significance? Michael Jordan playing his last game or a cocaine user for seven years with the cocaine destroying his marriage giving it up because he found Jesus?

When I drive by the stadium or a church and I hear a thundering sound coming from the sports house and the church house, I understand why both crowds get happy. One is emotional about a star and the other about a Savior.

(10) SPORTS

Looking at sports, I continue to be reminded of the concerns that ministers in Baltimore and St. Louis had when their two cities were bidding for football teams in their cities. They were concerned about the impact that football would have on their congregations and their contributions.

One possible remedy to the problem would be to attend an early morning worship service, since very few games are played at 6, 7 and 8 a.m. Large numbers of churches offer sunrise services at 6, 6:30, 7 or 8 a.m. If the man's major concern is that he wouldn't mind going to church if he could also be involved with sports, whether it be watching or playing a game, this has been solved. Also, very few bowling leagues or basketball games or tennis games are played at 6, 6:30, 7 and 8 a.m. Another possible suggestion is for the church to form sports ministries. At our church we have Athletes of Christ, and frequently, immediately after service, those men who want to play golf, bowl, or play tennis or basketball leave church to play. The same thing could also be done for those men who were interested in watching the game. Just as we go to bars to watch games, we could fellowship together after church in a room with a large-screen TV set, have snacks and watch the game together. Another suggestion is if there's a particular game you wanted to watch and there is a church activity creating a time conflict, you can tape the game. With my schedule I tape frequently, and what I enjoy about it is that I can watch the game without any commercials, time-outs or halftimes. I can watch a three-hour game in one hour. Beyond the technical issue of whether sports are preventing African American men from attending church, I just want to raise a personal question: Can Michael Jordan do for you what Jesus can? Did Michael Jordan die for you? Is Jordan always available when you need him? When you are in grave danger, do you call on Jordan? When you need someone to talk to in the wee hours of the morning, when you have a wayward child, a mate that is using drugs, and a marriage on the ropes, when you need a job, do you call on Jordan? Is Jordan coming back for you? We need to be clear about our priorities and they surely should not involve which one you're going to worship Sunday morning at 11 a.m.

(11) ATTIRE/DRESS CODE

It is unfortunate that many people believe you have to wear your Sunday finest in order to attend church. As the Christian community we have to ask ourselves, why do some think that way? Is that sentiment correct? If we become honest with ourselves and imagine what would it be like attending church if we did not have a suit, sport jacket, or nice dress to wear, how would we feel and do we think people would be looking at us in disdain? Nowhere in the Bible does the Lord give a criterion of how people should dress when they go to church. There are people and denominations that have attempted to do that, but the dress code does not come from Jesus. I have seen nationwide three interesting phenomena relating to the dress code.

The first one was in St. Louis. I was conducting a revival and I was very impressed with the pastor's ministry. He mentioned to me that he had relaxed the dress code and that brothers and sisters could dress casually. He encouraged his deacons and trustees to follow him in wearing pants, shirts, and sweaters, but not suits and sports jackets. He said the male population increased triplefold and that was the only variable altered. Many women inside the church were amazed at the increase resulting from the simple gesture of relaxing the dress code. Many middle-income people simply are not aware that not everyone owns a sport jacket or suit. Some people who have them are not comfortable wearing them. And if we are honest, for most of us, the first thing we do when we come home from church is take those clothes off and wear clothes that are more comfortable.

Second, I've seen churches during the summer months, especially those without air conditioning, relax the dress code. What sense does it make in rural Mississippi, in a church without air conditioning, for the men to wear suits and ties? Last, I've seen Africentric churches, including my own, encourage members to wear African dress. Many churches have people wear it on special occasions, while other churches have chosen certain weeks each month. I think this is an excellent idea, and obviously for one who is Africentric, I'm a major supporter. But again, I don't want people to feel that if they can't afford to buy African dress - because unfortunately African artifacts and African dress are often overpriced - they can't attend church. Many of the outfits are simple to make, and many European outfits can be complemented with kinte cloth. The major objective is that attire should not be a factor in a person's attendance and comfort level in the house of the Lord. The pastor needs to do whatever is necessary to achieve this goal.

(12)   CLASSISM/UNEMPLOYMENT

In 1920, 90 percent of African American youth had their fathers at home, and most of the men were working on farms or in factories. In 1960, 80 percent of African American youth had their fathers at home and they were primarily working in factories. Unfortunately, in the 1990s only 38 percent of African American children have their fathers at home and 25 percent of African American males are unemployed, because plants have closed and the jobs are now overseas. The question that the African American church needs to raise is, what position and what provisions are being made to address the change in the economy and reduce its impact on the African American male?

African American people were brought to this country to work. That reason no longer exists. White America raises the question, "What do we do with African American people we no longer need?" The question I'm raising to the church is, "What is your response to the change in the economy?" In earlier books, I've raised the questions, Can a man be a man in America without a job? Can a man be a man without a source of income? Will a man feel comfortable attending church without money? Is the church a middle-class institution? Do the homeless, the unemployed, the underemployed, and welfare recipients feel comfortable in church?

The Nation of Islam aggressively seeks these people on the streets, bars, and prisons. They not only share the Qur'an and Allah with the inmates, but upon acceptance provide them with a suit, newspapers, bean pies, fish, and Power products to sell. The question I'm raising to the church is, what does the Christian church provide? What economic opportunities does the Christian church provide for unemployed and underemployed African American men in the community? Prayer tickets?

The least the church could do is allow brothers to sell chicken dinners to the larger community after service. One minister during the summer identified a high school in South Central Los Angeles which had developed a salad dressing and during the summer made that product available to young people who couldn't find jobs. Another minister told me that when his youth couldn't find work during the summer, he helped them to develop greeting cards. That developed into a full-fledged business that has now become very lucrative. In order to attract more African American men to church, I recommend that churches provide counseling, résumé development, interview training, employment training, computer literacy classes, and placement. The church, like the Urban League, needs to gain the confidence of corporate America that their jobs can be filled satisfactorily.

(13) EDUCATION AND ILLITERACY

Many pastors and church parishioners may not know what it means to be illiterate in church. Every pastor and church member should imagine sitting in the pews and being illiterate and not being able to read the church bulletin, liturgy, and hymnals. The sermon may contain words the undereducated might not comprehend. I think that once we place ourselves in that position, we may alter our worship service. The church should be designed so that a person on ADC without a degree would be comfortable.

This is imperative within the context that 42 percent of African American youth can't read beyond a sixth-grade level. The disproportionate number of African American males in special education and dropping out exacerbates this problem. I often remind teachers that many times low-income single parents are uncomfortable talking with them because they use words parents may not understand and have a condescending, arrogant tone. The church needs to ask, "Did they really want to communicate with that person, and if they did, why did they choose to have a message given using 16-letter words?"

The church needs to develop programs for GED and literacy training that will provide an opportunity for people to improve their educational skills, not only to enjoy the worship service, as they enter and compete in the marketplace. I wonder how many African American churches provide literacy training or make referrals to other locations. The African American church should not be an institution like the newspaper where sixth-grade reading level is a prerequisite.

(14) SEXUALITY AND LIQUOR

I have acquaintances whose attendance is vacillating. They've told me that they're still young and they want to have fun, and that I should understand because I'm older. I assume they mean that when you're older, you don't want or need to have fun anymore, and because they are younger, they deserve to have fun. After they have enough fun and prepare for death, they will then confess their sins to God and begin to attend church and prepare for eternity in heaven. I asked them to define what they meant by fun. Janet Jackson defines fun as *anytime* and *anyplace*, to have sex when you want it, where you want it, and with whomever. It means being able to party as late as they want and come in after having breakfast at 7 a.m., when it's obvious that they are not going to the 8 or 11 a.m. service. And here's a reminder, some churches have Sunday evening services for people that worked, partied or were watching games during midday.

Another myth and misconception is that once you are saved and give your life to Christ, you no longer smile, laugh, party, dance, play cards and have enjoyable activities with friends. Myths and misconceptions don't exist in a vacuum. I've seen people become saved and so Africentric they convert joy and happiness into drudgery and boredom. I believe there are two things good for the soul: laughter and crying. I believe men who don't laugh and cry are suicidal. I read in my Bible that salvation and fun are not incompatible. I document that our Lord and Savior did have a good time. He enjoyed company and being in fellowship with friends and loved ones. I showed them that Jesus Christ went to a wedding, and when they had exhausted the wine, He turned water into wine for the party to continue. Not only did he enjoy weddings, but He also attended barbecues. Jesus Christ put fish on a charcoal grill and enjoyed himself out in the summer breeze at a barbecue. He enjoyed visiting friends like Martha and Mary with some of his disciples and just "kicking it around." We can praise God with all types of cymbals and sounds. We can praise God through song, dance and music.

A health study on people living in France documented that the French consume many products that are high in cholesterol, but they have a low incidence of heart disease. Further studies showed that there were three differences between their lifestyles and Americans. The first was that, unlike Americans, who may shop for the month and eat many foods processed in cans and boxes, the French take the time to purchase fresh produce daily. Second, the French do not rush eating their meals. While Americans were rapidly consuming hot dogs and french fries (in all of 5 minutes), people in France were taking an average of an hour. The third factor was a daily glass of wine. I know some people will use this study and Jesus turning water into wine as an excellent rationale for continuing their liquor consumption. African Americans are only 12 percent of the U.S. population, yet consume 39 percent of the liquor. One glass of fine wine occasionally may be OK for some people, but consuming a bottle of cheap wine daily is detrimental. Although some will rationalize that everything is OK *in moderation.* Moderation may seem logical, but how much crack cocaine consumption is OK? How much sex outside of marriage with someone who has AIDS is OK? How much stealing from a store in moderation is OK? How do you kill in moderation?

Alcohol consumption was a major reason not to go to church for African American men, but sexuality was greater. I have tremendous respect for A.C. Green, Barry Sanders, David Robinson, and numerous other brothers who have taken a strong stand for the Lord. A.C. Green speaks around the country and has developed a video titled *It Ain't Worth It* which promotes abstinence before marriage. The media will give more attention to Wilt Chamberlain, who said he was involved with at least 20,000 women and there is nothing that an African American woman can do for him, or Shaq saying that he doesn't like to read or watch network television, and if it's not on cable he won't watch it. But they give very little attention to David Robinson, who said, "I'm a Christian first, a scholar second, and a athlete third." When athletes confess Jesus as Lord, the media minimizes their coverage. I laugh when sports commentators interview athletes who are saved, because they want the athlete to give a technical explanation for the victory, and when athletes begin to testify about the Lord, they want to break immediately. It's OK to talk about your achievements and accomplishments as long as you give secular reasons, but when you start giving glory to God, the commentators want to take a commercial break.

African American female teenagers lead the world in teen pregnancy, and White American females would have led the world had it not been for abortions. Some schools distribute more condoms than books. It's encouraging that A.C. Green believes that abstinence should be taught before safer sex. Can you imagine what he endured when he was a member of the Los Angeles Lakers with teammates like Ervin "Magic" Johnson and James Worthy? Can you visualize the locker room when Magic is talking about how he's gonna have the thrill of his life with five sisters in the elevator? Or James Worthy calling in his sex order for two to perform his sexual fantasies? You can imagine how they dogged him in the locker room when he decided to spend the evening with Jesus.

This same scenario is played out in the regular locker rooms, where they dog any brother who talks about abstinence or prefers quality over quantity, a wife over a mistress. If you want to find out the psychological state of Black men, visit the locker room, barbershop or bar. There brothers brag about how many women they have and what women do for them, and any brother that doesn't agree is ostracized. When I'm in the locker room, I try to bond with the brothers while raising the level of consciousness. I ask myself, what would Jesus say to these Casanova brothers? I remember that when I was growing up I asked my father, why do women value the sexual act more than men? Why do women value their bodies more than men? Why do women seem to feel that their body is their greatest gift, and if they give themselves to you it is because they believe a commitment has been made, while it appears that men have no problems giving their bodies to whomever? Historically many people believed the reason for the difference was that women risk pregnancy every time they have intercourse. Therefore more was at stake and they sought commitment. With the onslaught of contraceptives, some women have the same value system that men have toward sex.

I have a colleague who tried to explain the difference in sexual orientation via anatomy. She said men have an external sexual organ, and females have an internal sexual organ, and the sexual act requires that he enters her. From a physiological perspective, she receives him and this creates emotions that make her dependent.

When I talk to male high school students, I remind them that they have two heads; one inside their pants and one on top of their neck. Which one is going to be in control? Many brothers are controlled by their penis and don't want pastors, who sometimes suffer from the same disease, telling them what they can or cannot do with it.

America reminds me of Sodom and Gomorrah. It reminds me of Rome. It has become obsessed with itself. America has become narcissistic. It is a country with only 6 percent of the world's population, but it consumes over 60 percent of the drugs.

(15) HOMOSEXUALITY

Word has it on the street, in the barbershop, in the bar and the locker room that the church is made up of elders, women, children and fags. This is a very sensitive area. I believe our socialization has failed many males. In Africa, manhood is based on the pyramid. African men must demonstrate a balance between the spiritual, mental and physical. Unfortunately, manhood in America is valued more from a physical perspective. Males are evaluated on how well they fight and play basketball, the number of women they have and babies made. Consequently, those males who value spirituality and have a personal relationship with God through Jesus Christ, who value academics

and the honor roll, who became engineers, surgeons, at-
torneys, and accountants, are not always accepted by their
male peer group. Those males who express themselves in
the fine arts, music, drama, and dance are often not accepted. I have noticed that many choirs have soprano,
alto, and tenor sections, but many don't have nor design
choral renditions with a baritone or bass section.

Many of these brothers are also rejected by their female peers. There are many elementary, high school, and
college female students who call them nerds and prefer
going out with a football or basketball player. They chose
the brother who talked back to the teacher and spent more
time on the streets than in his books. Now the young lady
has grown up and become mature. She's now in my workshop at the age of thirty, asking, where are the BMS/BMW/
BMC and BMEs?

I remember a parent and staff member in my talent center, where we tutor children and provide enrichment activities, ask me why I had a male homosexual tutoring their
children in math and science. I asked the parents whether
the teacher had put his hands on a child. Had he said
anything disrespectful? They said no. I said, "I'm very
much aware that this staff person is gay, but I did not hire
him because of his sexual orientation; he's a brilliant
mathematician, and your children needed assistance in al-
gebra and geometry. You and I both know that under his
tutelage your children are now doing very well and understand the concepts. African Americans have too many
needs for me to be narrow-minded and not allow someone
within our race who has the skills to correct a deficiency
not to be utilized."

The same applies to the church. The church needs deacons, trustees, teachers, counselors, singers, musicians,
and people to feed the hungry and clothe the naked. The
church is a hospital for sinners, not a museum for saints.
There are horror stories of AIDS victims who got AIDS
through their homosexual involvement, who have been

written off by the church and their own family members, who said, "That's what you deserve and this is God's wrath." This reminds me of the Scriptures describing the adulteress whom the men wanted to stone to death. Remember, you can't be an adulteress by yourself. There should have been at least one other person to be stoned. Jesus, not the Church or the crowd, said, "Let the person who has not sinned throw the first stone." The Scripture says the elders walked away first. It appears the longer you live, the longer you sin.

The one place where everyone should feel comfortable is the church. Homosexuals, adulterers and all other sinners should be accepted in the church. I'm sure that the homosexual community believes that their lifestyle is not sinful and was not a result of nurture and the socialization process but is one of nature and has a biological genesis. The homosexual community, which is politically well grounded and very astute, is doing everything within its power to promote that position. While I would take the position that all of us are sinners saved by grace, homosexuals who used to make that argument now argue that this lifestyle is not immoral and it is not sinful. This is where I disagree, but this should not deter African American men who have their own skeletons in the closets from being involved in the church.

I don't see African American men quitting their jobs because homosexuals are on the staff. Nor do I see men not watching or playing sports because some of the players are gay. Brothers, homosexuals are everywhere, so please don't use that as an excuse for not going to church.

(16) SPIRITUALITY/ UNIVERSALISM/WORSHIPING

In the last chapter I mentioned that some brothers distinguish between spirituality and religion. For many brothers, the argument is that they do not need organized religion to live right and practice morals, ethics, values,

Maat or the Nguzo Saba. I would agree. You do not need to physically be in a building Sunday at 11 a.m. following one man or denomination's interpretation and giving 10 percent of your income to an institution in order to have sound morals. My response to this argument is, "How much can one individual do to make a change in this world, and what other activities do you pursue individually?" Stokely Carmichael says in his speeches that we need to be organized. Every individual needs to become a member of an organization, and if your ego is so large that you have not found an organization that best represents your views, then start another organization and attract new members. If all African American people were members of organizations, their leaders could meet and develop policies and strategies that would benefit the entire race.

There is something beneficial about being part of a group. I have noticed that because of ego problems, many African American men are more effective when they are the only adult in the program, e.g., when they are a Little League baseball coach or Boy Scout leader. In this format, they make all the decisions and they can run the program to their choosing. Some men don't do as well in organizations like Rites of Passage or crime watch groups, where there are larger numbers of men working together.

The Lord said, "If two or three are gathered in my name, there I will be also." There is power in numbers. There is power in unity. There is power in fellowship. While a person may be able to develop a vertical relationship with the Lord by himself or herself, the horizontal relationship of reaching out to the larger community requires more than one person. And even the vertical relationship could be strengthened if you had the opportunity to be around fellow believers who had their own testimony to share about what the Lord has done in their lives. Many times just being around other people and listening to their testimony strengthens your own belief system.

That can't be secured if you are in communion with the Lord all by yourself. The significance of the church is not just to continue to develop a personal relationship with the Lord. But just as students come together to study before a large exam, just as adults come together to pool their resources to start a business, fellow believers understand that one benefit of the church is to come together to help *the least of these*. They realize that they will be more effective feeding the hungry, clothing the naked, providing back-to-school cultural programs, becoming tutors, teaching test-taking skills, offering scholarships, becoming role models, developing rites of passage programs, and all the other ministries that we need, if they do it collectively.

When an issue is being discussed I believe it's best to first find out what the Lord says. What did/would the Lord do? People need to ask themselves where was Jesus at the age of twelve when Mary and Joseph realized that their son was not with them; where did they find Him? He was in the Temple. And He said, "Upon this rock I will build My church."

Many church members could benefit from brothers who are serious about their spirituality and those seeking universal truth. I have seen brothers read their sacred texts at home much more diligently than some Christians. Many brothers want a more in-depth understanding of the Scriptures than an emotional worship service and brief superficial sermon may offer. In a scenario provided in an earlier chapter, my neighbor was at home on Sunday morning involved in an extensive comparative study of religions. He concluded that they all have something to offer and wanted to benefit from all of them. He wanted to exclude the bureaucracy, rigidity, pompous formality, and hierarchal disposition that only one religion is correct.

Many church members depend upon the pastor for their only religious experience of the week. Most pastors remind their congregation that they come to church on

Sunday for dessert, but the meal is provided through your daily walk with the Lord, reading Scripture and attending Bible classes where issues brothers are grappling with individually can be discussed collectively.

One of the things you notice immediately when you visit Africa is that there is no separation between Africans' spiritual life and their secular life, in contrast to America, where people seem to live sinfully for six days of the week and on the seventh day, for only two hours, they become holy. This is a society where people while in church can have people killed, rationalize slavery, and use ships named Jesus to take people from their homeland. The worship service should be a culmination of your weekly walk with the Lord, and with fellow believers you can celebrate how good the Lord has been to you this week. It is also a place where when you feel weak, you have fellow believers who will share your burdens, and you can draw upon their strength. The church could benefit from collective study and fellowship.

(17) HEAVEN

Many male critics of the church believe that there is too much emphasis on Heaven and life in the hereafter and not enough emphasis on enjoying life on earth. Many males are critical of pastors who teach them to   suffer today for a greater life tomorrow, while the pastor enjoys a good and better lifestyle on earth than his/her parishioners. They teach us that the last shall go first and the first shall go last, but some pastors seem to be first in the Cadillac line.

O.J. Simpson is a case in point; many people around the country comment to me, "I don't understand him: he had everything, a mansion, several cars, and business investments worth $10 million." I then ask them, "Who was O.J.'s God? Did $10 million make him happy?" I have seen people secure trinkets of Western materialism,

106

such as a Mercedes, and asked, "Is that all?" They possessed the finest wardrobe and again asked, "Is that all?" They purchased a mansion and asked, "Is that all?" They bought a yacht and again asked, "Is that all?" With each trinket they thought it would make them happy, only to find out that the void remained. It's difficult for poor people to imagine that material things will not make them happy. You have many rich people raising the question, "Is this all?" And you have many poor people saying, I don't understand O.J., he had everything.

Scripture taken out of context says that the love of money is the root of all evil. Properly understood this means not money in and of itself, but how money is valued is the root of all evil. When the rich man asked the Lord, "What good thing must I do to receive eternal life?" the Lord answered, "Give up your possessions and follow me." The significance of that question is just like the significance of the Lord asking Abraham to sacrifice his son Isaac. What is it that you value so much that it would affect your desire to do what the Lord wanted you to do? Is there anything that you value more than your relationship with the Lord? That becomes your Isaac, and for most of us, our money and our desire for Western materialism circumvents our relationship with the Lord. Money is not the root of all evil, but money is an evil if it prevents you from having a relationship with God. Money is evil if you hoard it and keep it from the *least of these*. There is nothing wrong with being rich. There were many people in the Bible who were rich. The man who wanted eternal life was rich. Many of the disciples that followed Jesus were rich. They were entrepreneurs who had their own fishing companies with paid employees and were able to leave their fishing companies and follow Jesus because their businesses had astute managers.

The question of eternity, a belief in life after death, a belief that Heaven is real, has its genesis in Africa, not Europe. The symbol of Maat is represented by a feather

placed on one scale and your life's work on the other scale.
The day of judgment should reflect that your wrongs did
not exceed the weight of the feather. One of the cardinal
virtues of Maat is balance. From a time perspective, life
on earth is minuscule when compared to eternal life. We
are only here for a moment in God's eyes, approximately
70 years, to make this world a better place and be remembered forever. When you look at it from God's perspective, the accent should be on eternal life, not temporal
life.

In the spirit of Maat, an overemphasis on eternal life to
the detriment and denial of life on earth is unbalanced. If
Jesus did not believe in taking care of peoples' physical
needs, He would not have fed over 20,000 people (5,000
men plus women and children). He could have said, "I'm
sorry but you need to go without today; there is food waiting for you in Heaven." Instead, He fed them on earth.

Men have a valid criticism if they feel that entertainment and containment churches are not addressing the
needs of people on earth. We need all churches, 75,000
of them, to practice liberation theology. Isaiah 58 requires
us to fast, sacrifice, feed the hungry and clothe the naked.
Many Christians have resolved the tomorrow question, but
haven't addressed today's question. Many brothers outside the church have resolved today's question, but not
tomorrow's question.

(18) LACK OF EVANGELISM

I believe you can't criticize someone for not being
involved if the person has never been asked. In the
previous chapter we mentioned that many brothers have
commented that they have seen the hypocrisy and the class
divisiveness of the African American church. Some
churches minister to elders before youth, women before
males, the middle class before the underclass. The group
that seems to be ignored the most is young African

American males that make up what Julius Wilson describes as the underclass.

The church is designed like so many social agencies with excellent programs and resources; they have the answers but an inadequate outreach ministry. I don't think that design is by accident. When you observe the majority of institutions, they are structured this way. Lack of outreach has become the norm. They are more comfortable staying inside their buildings with the resources and sharing them only with people who seek their services. The church needs a greater marketing/advertising thrust.

If we really believe in our program, we need to take it to the street. One thing I respect about Jehovah's Witnesses is that as much as I resent their knocking on my door, it is obvious from their outreach perserverance that they believe in their program. Outreach ministry was the cornerstone in Marcus Garvey's organizing almost a million African Americans without television. The Black church can't have it both ways. Pastors can't ask where the brothers are in the comfort of the sanctuary while driving by them and not offering programs and ministries. There's a joke in the Black community that White people rise earlier than African Americans, and when African American people finally wake up, they ask what happened? The parallel also exists between Christians and Muslims. Some Christians are asking, "Where are the brothers?" Meanwhile Muslims continue meeting them where they are. They know exactly where they are. Many of them were in those same places just a few days, weeks and months ago. Some Christians get saved and get amnesia about where the Lord met them, in a bar, in jail or on the street corner. Many inmates are also witnessed by male Muslims or White female Christians.

(19) LACK OF CHRISTIAN ROLE MODELS

While the aggregate numbers for church attendance have increased, because the total African American population is increasing, church start-ups do not mean that the percentage of churchgoers has increased. I previously stated that in 1940, 80 percent of African American families attended church. That percentage has declined to 40 percent five decades later. It is now possible that larger numbers of African American children, specifically male, have grown up in households where there has not been one saved male in the household. Many boys have not known a saved, churchgoing male in their extended family, which includes grandfathers, uncles, brothers, nephews, cousins, and mother's boyfriends. In contrast, African American females knew a greater number of female extended family members who were saved and attended church. Many times during the year the pastor will ask the congregation to bring a brother, especially if it's men's week. I know I've been guilty of not putting tremendous effort into that request. I briefly think of brothers I know who are not in church, but I need to spend more time calling them and if necessary providing transportation. I am appealing to all readers to develop a list of twenty brothers who are not attending church and invite them to worship. Many brothers have not had a male witness to them about the goodness of Jesus.

We need to invite them to a liberation church, where most of the reasons African American males don't attend are being resolved. The last thing we want is to take them to a entertainment or containment church, where all the reasons given for not attending are present.

(20) STREETS AND PEER PRESSURE

Many brothers have said they feel a greater camaraderie with the brothers on the street than in the church. They come from the same cloth and understand each other. Their bond is being the victim of White male supremacy, regardless of their understanding. John Perkins describes brilliantly how Jesus met the Samaritan woman at the well. He portrays it in three stages: relocation, redistribution, and reconciliation. While He was in the temple at 12 years of age, He didn't stay in the church. He took His ministry into communities where *the least of these* lived and met the Samaritan woman where she was--at the well. This was opposed and not accepted by the established religious community. Christ and the Church do not always have the same agenda. The first significant point is relocation. He left the church and met her where she was--at the well. The African American church has to meet brothers where they are, and large numbers of them are on the street. The second stage was redistribution. Jesus met her at the well and then asked her for a drink of water. You would think that someone who can turn water into wine and can walk on water could have easily secured his own cup of water, but He wanted to empower her. He wanted her to feel important and realize she had skills and resources that He needed. He wanted to redistribute the power and self-esteem. He wanted the brothers on the street to be empowered and made to feel important. The brothers on the street have skills and resources that the church needs. They have been written off by the larger society and, unfortunately, by many churches.

The Samaritan woman, like our street brothers, had been written off by society, but the Lord still loved her. He forgave her and loved her unconditionally. He wanted to show her that He loved her unconditionally. The church needs to do that, because many of our brothers are crying on the inside.

Many street brothers have moved to the first state called denial. They fear confronting their pain. They immerse themselves in a peer group where misery loves company. Their fellowship and communication is on the corners, where they sip wine and pay libations out of brown paper bags. It's obvious that they believe in fellowship or they would not be with each other. We need to reconcile ourselves to them.

(21) DOUBLE STANDARDS/FORCED WHEN A CHILD

I have written in *Countering the Conspiracy to Destroy Black Boys* that mothers' double standards are almost as dangerous to the development of African American males as White supremacy, absentee fathers and lower teacher expectations. Many church going mothers often ask me, "Where is Adam?" Normally *Adam Jr.* is at home watching television while she and his sister are attending church. I believe the relationship between some mothers and sons plummets into a girlfriend-boyfriend relationship. Sons are often like boyfriends when it comes to believing their mother, e.g., the girlfriend is nagging both of them. The mother-girlfriend begins to acquiesce and allows the son-boyfriend to make his own decisions. The desire for peace supersedes what is correct.

I asked the brothers how many of them were parents. The entire group raised their hands. I didn't ask them whether they were living with their children or were in regular communication with them. I did ask them, "Do you give your children an option on going to school? Do you give them an option of wearing a coat rather than a sweater when it's cold outside? Do you let your children eat dessert when they didn't eat their dinner? Do you let your children stay up late when they have school in the morning? Then why do you feel it should be optional to go to church to learn morality?"

Women and men, can you explain why more African American females graduate from high school and college than African American males? Is the only answer institutional racism? Could African American females be more responsible and focused? Why do more African American males kill African American males than African American females kill African American females? Are the answers only guns, drugs and power? Could African American females be more forgiving? They forgive brothers almost every day. Why do African American females commit suicide less than anyone else? Do they have more hope? Are they stronger? What makes them so strong? Did their mothers make them attend church?

When Black men walk with Jesus, they are not afraid of taking back their streets.

CHAPTER SEVEN
Models of Ministry

I mentioned earlier that there is at least one liberation church in every major city in America. In many cities there are several churches that have a liberation theology and for that reason have been able to attract a larger number of men and youth. While the male percentage is higher in liberation churches, there are few churches out of 75,000 with a larger percentage of men than women. There are churches where men makeup nearly 40 percent of the congregation. I could list these churches and their pastors because I know most of them and have spoken before them. I choose not to mention the names of the churches and pastors because invariably, you omit a few. Second, books, unlike newspapers and magazines, should transcend time. It would be laborious with each reprinting to chronicle the movement of pastors and their churches. For example, I could have written this book in a particular year, and my friend Frank Reid would have been listed at Ward AME Church in Los Angeles. But because I'm writing the book this year, he is at Bethel AME Church in Baltimore.

Liberation churches have a male population that exceeds 25 to 30 percent, have ministries for males, and have study sessions where these 21 reasons and more have been discussed. These congregations and pastors know whether they have a liberation church. Hopefully, people who recognize these churches will gravitate to them or recreate them. I pray that those pastors of entertainment and containment churches will pray for a vision to design ministries that will be attractive to African American men.

The Scriptures that I think best exemplify manhood and what the Lord said to men to inspire and motivate men have been carefully selected and are offered to consider in various men's programs throughout the year. I'm sure many pastors have already used these Scriptures at one time or another to exalt, exemplify and challenge Black manhood. In the order in which they are presented in the Bible, the first Scripture is the title of this book, Genesis 3:9. The Lord God called out to the man, "Where are you, where are you Adam?" The second Scripture, Numbers 11:26, is used by a liberation church in New York to form their male ministry. "Two of the seventy male leaders, Eldad and Medad, had stayed in the camp and had not gone out to the tent. There in the camp the spirit came on them and they too began to shout like prophets." The next Scripture comes from the Book of Judges, when the Lord, like the Marines, is looking for a few good men. Judges 7:7: The Lord said to Gideon, "I will rescue you and give you victory over the Midianites with the 300 men who lapped the water. Tell everyone else to go home." The next Scripture describes the strength of African men. If African people were inferior, there would be no need to discriminate. When African men have the opportunity to compete, they win. African American males have become the best surgeons and basketball players, which demonstrates strength on both the right and left side of the brain. The Scripture is Judges 16:15-17: "So Delilah said to Samson, 'Please tell me what makes you so strong.'" She kept asking him, day after day. He got so sick and tired of her bothering him about it that he finally told her the truth. "My hair has never been cut," he said. "I have been dedicated to God as a Nazirite from the time I was born. If my hair were cut, I would lose my strength and be as weak as anybody else."

The next Scripture is Isaiah 3:4-5: The Lord will let the people be governed by immature boys. We now live in a world of drive-by shootings. We live in communities where young boys now think they are in charge. When I was growing up and we were playing in the park and there was a skirmish, there were adult men in the park who were available and willing to resolve it. Today, in most neighborhoods, parks, and on the streets, when there are skirmishes you can't find adult men. Therefore young boys between eleven and nineteen believe they are in charge. You read Isaiah 3:4 and feel that you're reading a contemporary newspaper. Another powerful scripture is John 11:39-43, where a parallel is made between Lazarus and African American males.

The last Scripture I want to suggest is Ephesians 5:25, 28, 31. It has amazed me how brothers who do not attend church seem to know Ephesians 5:22-23 but not 25, 28, and 31. Ephesians 22-23 reads: "Wives submit yourselves to your husbands as unto the Lord. For a husband has authority over his wife just as Christ has authority over the church." It is amazing how brothers who are not in church, who don't believe the Bible, know that Scripture by heart and are quick to tell their women that they need to submit, obey, and accept that the man as the head of the house. First, Scripture should always be read in context. Verses should not be extracted one at a time to reinforce a position. If brothers read further, they will receive a much broader understanding. Ephesians 25 reads: "Husbands love your wives just as Christ loved the Church and gave his life for it." Verse 28 continues, "Men ought to love their wives just as they love their own bodies. A man who loves his wife loves himself." And for those brothers who want to continue to live with their parents and never break the umbilical cord, Ephesians 31 reminds us: "For this reason a man will leave his father and mother and unite with his wife and the two will become one." Scripture can be our inspiration to ministries that will bring Black men together to inspire them, to empower them to make our families, our churches, our neighborhoods, and our communities stronger.

117

Observing churches, whether they are entertainment, containment, or liberation, almost all will allocate at least one day of the year to empower the African American male. Traditionally it's been called Men's Day. In most churches, on Men's Day, the men will sing. There will be a special guest male preacher, politician, or famous male speaker. The pastor may ask all the men in the sanctuary to stand and ask the remaining congregation to applaud them. I observed one church that did this and when the men stood up it was very impressive. I wanted to tell the sisters, who always ask me where the brothers are, "look at these fine men standing up for the Lord." The church held 1,000 people, 300 of which were men. On this particular Sunday, after the men stood, the pastor asked them to sit down, and for whatever the reason, asked the women to stand, and then it was very difficult to see the men. There were some pews that were completely filled with women. While seeing 300 men was impressive, in large churches, if the percentage remains 30 percent, we still have 400 women without a mate in the church.

There have been two interesting phenomena I've observed about Men's Day that I have been pondering. The first is that you would think that on Men's Day every effort would be made to have the congregation all bring one man to church, especially the existing men in the church. If the church had 300 men, you'd like to believe that on Men's Day, potentially it could have 600 men worshiping and praising God. I believe the church missed a prime opportunity to evangelize and witness to men.

The second observation is the heavy emphasis on raising money; primarily men raising money from women. It appears that Men's Day has become one of the major fund-raisers. I wouldn't have a problem with Men's Day being used as a fund-raiser if the money donated were going to address the unique problems African American men are experiencing. Can you imagine what would happen if a church raised money for Men's Day and directed the proceeds to address the problem by purchasing wholesale products that men could sell at retail prices? Can you imagine if the monies raised were used to provide drug treatment? Can you imagine what would happen if the money raised was used to build a family life center (for recreational and educational purposes)? Some churches have done just that.

Some Congress persons felt that midnight basketball was pork in the crime bill, and their commentary and their cynicism about basketball deterring crime does an injustice to the bill. Large numbers of prisoners were on street corners between 10 p.m. and 3 a.m. Many older adults acknowledge when they were growing up, there were recreational opportunities and facilities for them that no longer exist for the current generation. The first objective is to take young people off the street in these critical hours. Second, midnight basketball is simply used as a carrot. All participants that play basketball agree to be tutored, to pursue their GED and to have job training. Some legislators seem to think that the solution to the crime problem is to provide more metal detectors in school, more police on the street, more prisons, and longer sentences with less emphasis on self-esteem, Africentricity, tutoring, recreation and economic development. These provisions are cheaper and cost-effective. When I was in college I wondered if America's powerbrokers didn't know that Head Start, Chapter I, Pell Grants and job training were more effective than building prisons. When I became older I realized that they did know, but the objective was never to empower African American people, it was to oppress them at whatever cost. Therefore, I spend less time trying to convince oppressors of the validity of Head Start, Chapter I, Pell Grants, job training and midnight basketball and more time appealing to pastors of entertainment and containment churches to consider using the funds collected in the name of Men's Day to address the problems of African American men.

The male model of ministry programs is being presented in the order which I think reflects their seriousness and commitments. While I commend churches for having Men's Day services, I believe that men need far more than one day out of 365 days to address their problems. This is similar to schools that teach African history one month a year, and ironically it's the shortest month. I do feel it's a step in the right direction. A greater commitment to African American men would be Men's Week or Men's Revival. There are churches nationwide that have transcended a one-day observation and have chosen to make the entire week an opportunity to inspire African American men. Unfortunately, churches still have a seventy-to-thirty female-to-male ratio at these weekly activities.

There are some churches that also provide male-only workshops. I think this is significant, because many times during Men's Week or revival the sermons don't always address issues facing African American men. This may be because the revivalist during Men's Week is still speaking to a congregation 70 percent female. This week of activities is also designed to raise funds for the church. I have the same criticism as I had of Men's Day. I seldom hear the pastor indicating that the funds collected will be used to address the problems of African American men.

The next activity I have observed has been a men's retreat. What makes this significant and shows the vision and leadership of the pastor is that he/she wants to take the men away from their normal habitat and allow a change in scenery. The retreat allows only men to attend. The Nation of Islam understands the value of separating males from females for a myriad of reasons. One of the primary reasons is that men act differently if they are in the presence of women; their conversation and focus are different, their attention oftentimes is diverted, and their egos motivate them to try to impress women. Men's retreat allows them to come together, sometimes for the very first time, and cry, share their most intimate secrets with one another, form a cadre and experience camaraderie they have never experienced. Every man owes it to himself to experience being in a room for a weekend with 25 to 500 or more men. It is powerful. I've also experienced being with large groups of men for athletics, scholarship and Africentricity. But of all the male gatherings, being in a room filled with God-fearing men who are filled with the Holy Spirit is a indescribable feeling. These retreats offer Bible study, prayer, workshops, athletics, sermons, music, and intimate sharing. Some churches have used Africentric publications including *Visions of Black Manhood* by Na'im Akbar, Earl Hutchinson's books, the *Assassination of the Black Male Image and Black Fatherhood*, and my collection of *Countering the Conspiracy to Destroy Black Boys, Volumes, 1 through 4.*

The next activity is a monthly men's fellowship, which shows an even greater level of commitment to bring Black men together and begin to address some of the problems that African American men are experiencing. Unlike a special activity for a day or a week, or an annual retreat, this activity meets monthly. It brings men together, with the major components being fellowship, Bible study, prayer concerns and responsibilities to the church. This group is normally involved in the admi-nistration of Men's Day, Men's week or a Men's retreat. Men's fellowships create special outings for the men, including golf, bowling, tennis or some other activities to create camaraderie. Unfortunately the group seems very provincial; an outreach ministry seldom is on the agenda. The age demographics of the group, especially the leadership, is generally over 45 years of age.

Sisters looking for marriageable brothers between the ages of 21 and 45 may find very few at Mens' Fellowship. Mens' Fellowship is not the training grounds for young men to learn their manhood, because of the tremendous age range. Men outside the church who need to experience the joy of Jesus Christ may not attend this fellowship because of the lack of solicitation and evangelism. Young men under forty-five may not be encouraged to be in leadership positions. Oftentimes elders say the youth are the future, but the proof of that statement will be when elders allow young people to have a greater level of responsibility in the ministries in which they participate.

The next ministry which shows a greater level of commitment to empower African American men would be a weekly Bible study. This group meets on a weekly basis to study the Word of God. The numbers at the weekly Bible study class are usually smaller then the numbers at the annual retreat. For many reasons, brothers seem to be able to make a commitment once a year, but on a weekly basis, the numbers decline. Regardless of whether the number is 2 or 200, the Lord says in His Word that if two or three are gathered in His name then He will be there also. Men's Bible Study class is a powerful experience to continue the fellowship men receive at the annual men's retreat.

The next ministry that I observed primarily at liberation churches is a weekly men's manhood class which combines Bible study with Africentricity. These groups not only meet on a weekly basis to study God's Word, but they also read some of the cultural books I cited earlier, along with various articles that the pastor and the planning committee feel would be helpful to African American men. When I have spoken at these classes, I've also noticed that there is a larger number of male visitors in these classes. There are numerous reasons why I think this occurred.

The grapevine informs unbelievers that all men are welcomed. Second, if you want to be with a group of men, who are looking at the issues of unemployment, crime, drugs, and family stability from an Africentric point of view that is biblically based, and admission is free, it's an excellent opportunity. Last, because the meeting is weekly rather than monthly, brothers are able to remember better, and if they miss one, there is always next week. I've seen visitors makeup anywhere from 1/10 to 1/3 of the audience. I've also seen not only unbelievers attend, but also members from other churches. There are two major concerns I have about this particular class. I think it's an excellent opportunity for men to come together biblically and secularly. Too many programs are either Christocentric or Africentric, but not both. One of the concerns is that these classes are normally led by the pastor, which in and of itself is not a problem, but I've noticed that if the pastor transfers the class to an assistant or if the group knows the pastor is going to be absent, the attendance wanes. It shows one of our major weaknesses: African Americans rely too much on the messenger rather than the message. Every effort should be made by the pastor to circumvent this. The pastor should announce we are here as men, not because of me, but to study God's Word and to appreciate our heritage. The pastor can reinforce this by being physically present but having other people lead the session. This can also be done at the Sunday worship service; the accent should be on Christ, not the pastor.

I believe one way to measure an effective leader is by how strong his or her second or third person is. This is also an excellent opportunity for second or third persons to rise to the surface and not simply be the speaker by default because the pastor is absent. I've seen men's classes dissolve when the class was no longer taught by the pastor.

The second observation I wanted to make about these men's classes, whether the class is weekly, men's Bible study, fellowship, men's week, or men's day, they all have one variable in common: the men in the audience are not expected to do anything except listen and talk. Even if the pastor has assigned reading material, many brothers don't read the materials, but think that they can rap their way through the entire discussion. My major concern about these above programs is that they do not require any work from the men. That may explain why the numbers are larger than for ministries that require work.

I observed one men's class that was both biblical and Africentric, and it was being conducted in a liberation church with a charismatic preacher. There were over 300 men having a good time talking and rapping about problems. A male member who was involved in a rites of passage program decided to "bust them out" that day. He came into the sanctuary where the meeting was taking place with about 24 African American boys that were members of the program. He was the only man with the group because the other three men who had agreed to work with the group had become inconsistent. The male member stood up and said, "I just want you to know that whenever you're ready to stop talking about the problems and what the solutions may be, I will gladly let you practice some of your theories, programs and solutions on these 24 boys you're looking at." I naively thought the men would respond to the challenge and join that ministry or a similar ministry and move from theory to practice, but they were so comfortable listening and rapping that those boys still need men. I continue to wrestle with that phenomenon. But at this point in my life, I realize that people do what they want to do. Behavior is louder than words. Those men were more comfortable sitting and talking about issues they have not read about and wishing that only the pastor would lead the session. These men want to be entertained, and that reflects the state of Black manhood even in some liberation churches.

The next ministries involve men who have gone beyond discussing the problem but now want to work. In the book of Nehemiah, we are charged to return home and rebuild walls. The first ministry we want to highlight is a role model or mentoring project. Some of these ministries even used Nehemiah as the name of their program. I observed one event where a church adopted a school in their local neighborhood. The pastor called a meeting. The pastor and the principal met and discussed the dearth of fathers in the home. The teaching staff consisted of 30 teachers, 28 females and two males. The boys needed role models. The boys needed to see African American men do more than hang out on corners, sell drugs, and play basketball. The pastor and principal agreed they would collaborate and work together. Before I spoke, the principal had the 200 boys line up in single file around the gymnasium and then the pastor led 200 men into the gym and each man stood in front of a boy. I then led a litany for the men.

The men said, "I promise to call you once a week. I promise to visit with you once a week. I promise to review your report card when it is released. I promise to stay in your life until you either go to college or become gainfully employed. I make this promise to you, I make this promise to the school. I make this promise to the church. I make this promise to God." The boys then responded, "I accept your promise, I look forward to your call. I look forward to spending time with you. I will do everything I can to make you proud of my report card. I will graduate from high school and I will do everything I can to go to college." The pastor and principal then said, if you do that, then we will do everything we possibly can to find the economic resources, if you do not receive a scholarship, for you to attend college. It was at that point I was supposed to speak. I just couldn't do it. The tears did not allow me to speak. Several times this has happened in my career. The tears became contagious, and the boys and men hugged each other. Have you ever seen 200 men hug 200 boys while crying?

I hope your church will consider developing a Nehemiah project, but don't start this program with inconsistent men. Our boys become very cynical. They have seen programs start and stop due to inconsistency.

They have seen adults become dependent on grants, and when they end so does the program. They have seen men make promises and not deliver. How can we expect a man to be a role model if he promised his child that he was going to pick him up at two in the afternoon and never showed up? That's why these classes I mentioned earlier are important, so when it's time to go out on the battlefield and begin to do God's work, we will be ready, prepared, and committed.

In the Nation of Islam, programs almost always start on time. Unfortunately, many Christian programs do not. What would have happened if the principal had escorted the 200 boys into the gym at 1 p.m. and the men had not arrived until 2 p.m.? Would the effect had been the same if only 100 men had showed up? What will the boys think if over the next few weeks the number of men declines? What lessons do men teach boys when they're inconsistent?

The next ministry is Rites of Passage. I feel this ministry is more intensive than the role model program because in the latter program, you have one man with one boy and the activities between each man and boy can be very diverse. It doesn't require Africentricity, which is why all people are eligible for role model programs. Rites of Passage requires a group of men to work with a group of boys following the same Africentric curriculum. The national Rites of Passage organization has created minimal standards that all programs are to adhere to. That does not exist in a role model program. These nine minimal standards include spirituality, history, economics, politics, community involvement, career development, physical development, family responsibility, and values.

The word *rites* is plural, which means that there are numerous Rites of Passage ceremonies that a male will experience. This prevents agencies that received a three-to-six-month grant from thinking they can bestow upon a twelve-year-old boy the honor of being a man. Boys may experience one level of rites at 12, another set at 16, and one at 18, 21 and 25; it is a continual process. One of the most enjoyable experiences I've had with Rites of Passage has been employing some of my Rites graduates in current Rites programs.

The last ministry is the one that requires the greatest level of commitment. I've also saved it for last because it means the most to me. It cannot be implemented unless men are serious. There's a tremendous difference in the level of commitment required to have an annual Men's Day program and having a crime watch group like Community of Men. This ministry requires a great deal of seriousness, because gang members and drug dealers are serious and heavily armed. I read in Isaiah 3:4, where these boys believe they are in charge.

The Community of Men is a group of men that come together to address the issues of crime, gangs and drugs in our neighborhoods. The objective is for the men to analyze, strategize, and identify crime-infested areas and begin to provide alternatives. When we started this ministry in 1992, there were 175 men there. It reminded me of Gideon, where there were 22,000. But when it came time to actually walk the streets, we declined to 68, and presently we have 21, and my father remains a member.

I'm very much aware that the Lord can with little, do much, and had we kept 175, like Gideon, we might have thought the victory was ours. The 175 was mostly fat; the 21 brothers represent muscle. Whatever victories we achieve now, we know they came from the Lord. It has also been challenging trying to keep the 21 men from burning out.

The issue of crime is so complex and interwoven that there are many different ways to attack it. Ideally speaking, America has the ability to take guns and drugs off the street. The wealthiest county could provide everyone that wanted a job with an adequate livable salary. If we could improve the quality of education, reducing the number of

African American males who fail kindergarten, their scores declining after fourth grade, and who are disproportionately placed in special education and unfairly suspended then reduction in the dropout rate, which hovers near 50 percent in most African American males in most urban areas, would also place a major dent in the crime problem. If we could match every boy with a role model and begin to mentor him and provide academic, cultural, and recreational opportunities to keep his mind active, we could reduce crime. If we could teach boys how to resolve conflict through nonviolence rather than with an AK47, we could also make a significant contribution.

Another way to address the crime issue in our community is to picket in front of stores that sell drug paraphernalia to our children and sell liquor and cigarettes to minors. We need to confront these business owners that are destroying our children. We need to monitor billboards in our communities that promote liquor and cigarettes. Community of Men decided they were going to identify drug and gang-infested neighborhoods. We were going to distribute literature on the sources of guns and drugs and their impact on our community. We would appeal to the men in the neighborhood we were marching to join us and take their own neighborhoods back. We requested assistance from parents to send their boys to the building that we secured that we were going to use to conduct academic, entrepreneurial, and recreational activities for their sons. Notice that marching through the neighborhood was designed only to inform the community about drugs and guns, recruit men, and advertise our program to parents. There are many institutions that have made marching through communities a lifetime experience. Sometimes I think gang bangers and drug dealers laugh at marchers, because they know the march will last only for a few hours. Some may take a nap or grab something to eat, because they know that after sundown, the streets belong to them.

I chose Monday night as the night that we would march through communities, stabilize buildings and provide academic and recreational and entrepreneur activities for young people, because that's the night I'm in town 95 percent of the time. If we were more committed and had more men, we would increase the number of nights and concentrate on Friday and Saturday nights. While our program is effective there are more incidents of crime on Friday and Saturday night. A liberation church in Pittsburgh said they had a similar ministry, and they patrol the streets on Saturday night.

There is a wide range of activities for men. In this chapter, I have attempted to show they range from an annual Men's Day activity to a crime watch group. One of the weaknesses of many Christian programs is the lack of accountability. When our members don't show up or call, we pray for them and hope to see them next week. I wonder if a member of the Fruit of Islam was not present, would they pray for him or prey on him. Grace and forgiveness are more important than the law, but we must begin to hold brothers accountable.

In conclusion, I have throughout this book raised the question, "Where are you Adam?" to 16 million African American men who are outside the Christian church. Black women are raising that question, because they are looking for a BMS, a Black man saved. Black children, especially Black boys, are raising that question, because they can't be a Black man without Adam. Black schools and Black organizations are raising the question because they know they can't run their Role Model, Rites of Passage and Community of Men without Adam.

Last, the focus for this book, the Black church, is raising the question because of the disproportionate ratio of females to males in the church. When figures reach this magnitude, we have to find the reasons why African American men have strayed away from church and what can be done to bring them back. This book has also been an attempt to challenge the four million brothers who are in the church and ask them, Where are you, Adam? When was the last time you witnessed Adam? When was the last time you spent quality time with a male child? When are you going to stop young boys from placing fear in the hearts and minds of elders and women and children? How tragic that we now live in a world where elders would rather die of a lack of ventilation in their houses during the summertime, than to open up their windows and run the risk of a Black male coming in and killing them. The African American community should have been up in arms when the queen of the civil rights movement, Rosa Parks, was attacked by Black male predators. We raise the question, Where are you Adam?

Finally, the Lord wants to ask Adam two very personal questions from His Word, Matthew 16: 13, 15. The Lord asks Adam, "Who do the people say that I am?" Who do your friends say that you run with, the brothers that you drink with, the brothers that you shoot up with, the brothers you play ball with. Who do they say that I am? Who do the rappers, the nationalists, the Muslims, who do the unbelievers say that I am. Who do your intellectual and scholarly friends say that I am? Adam answers, some say you are a prophet, but not the last one. Some say you are Michealangelo's fantasy or his cousin. Some say they are mad at you because you let them down. Some say you participated in the slave trade and the ship had your name. Some say you are a wimp. Some say your name is not Jesus, but Heru or Horus. Some say you are a great man who tried to do the right thing. Some say you are a fake and a phony and you just want everybody's money. The Lord says, I see. Adam, that was the preliminary question. That was the scholarly question. That was the question that you could answer in the third person. That was your mother or sister's answer. But the last question, Adam, only you can answer. This question, Adam, will be more personal. It will be the relationship question.

Adam, you don't have to answer if you aren't ready. But I'd like to know, Adam, who do you say that I am? When you are in trouble, when a car is dangerously approaching you, when you are lying on your back in the hospital, when you have tried all the secular options and you've called all of your friends and they're either busy or unable to meet you, where the bone meets the marrow, when your heart begins to hurt. You've been there, Adam, and when you were there, at that point, who do you say that I am?

This book began with scripture, just as in the beginning was the word and the word was God and the word became flesh. The first scripture described the first Adam. This last scripture finally answers the question, "Where is Adam?"

First Corinthians 15:45-47

For the scripture says, "The first man, Adam was created a living being," but the last Adam is the lifegiving Spirit. It is not the spiritual that comes first, but the physical, and then the spiritual. The first Adam, made of earth, came from earth; the second Adam came from heaven.

Appendix A

Adam's Responses

1. Hypocrisy
2. Ego/Dictatorial
3. Faith/Submission/Trust/Forgiveness/Anger
4. Passivity
5. Tithing
6. Irrelevance
7. Eurocentric
8. Length of Service
9. Emotional
10. Sports
11. Attire/Dress Code
12. Classism/Unemployment
13. Education/Literacy
14. Sexuality and Drugs
15. Homosexuality
16. Spirituality/Universalism/Worshiping Alone
17. Heaven
18. Evangelism
19. Lack of Christian Role Models
20. Streets/Peer Pressure
21. Double Standards/Forced when a Child

Appendix B

Recommended Readings

Na'im Akbar. *Visions for Black Men.* Winston-Derek Publishers, Nashville, TN, 1991.

James Anyike. *Historical Christianity African Centered.* Popular Truth, Chicago, IL, 1994.

Anthony Browder. *Nile Valley Contributions to Civilization.* Institute of Karmic Guidance, Washington D.C., 1992.

Cain Hope Felder. *Troubling Biblical Waters.* Orbis Books, Maryknoll, 1989.

Cain Hope Felder. Edited. *Stony the Road We Trod.* Fortress Press, Minneapolis, MN, 1991.

Robert Franklin. *"Reclaiming the Souls of Black Men Folk,"* Paper presented at Howard University One-third of a Nation Conference.

Samuel Freedman. *Upon This Rock.* Harper Collins, New York, N.Y., 1993.

William Harris. *"Why Most Black Men Won't Go to Church,"* *Upscale Magazine*, April/May 1990.

Yosef ben Jochannan. *African Origins of the Major Western Religions.* Alkebulan Books, New York, N.Y., 1970.

Jawanza Kunjufu. *Countering the Conspiracy to Destroy Black Boys* Volume I-IV, African American Images, Chicago, IL, 1995.

C. Eric Lincoln and Lawrence Mamiya. *The Black Church in The African American Experience*, Duke University Press, Durham, N.C., 1990.

C. Eric Lincoln. *The Black Muslims in America*, Africa World Press. Trenton, N.J., 1994.

Walter McCray. *The Black Presence in the Bible*, Black Light Fellowship, Chicago, IL, 1990.

Sylvester Monroe. "The Fruits of Islam." *Emerge Magazine*, March 1994.

William Mosley. *What Color Was Jesus?* African American Images, Chicago, IL, 1987.

Frank Reid. "Your Brother will Rise again: Reaching Black Men." *The Christian Ministry* November/December 1994 pp18-21.

Jeremiah A. Wright Jr. *What Makes You So Strong?* Judson Press, Philadelphia, PA, 1994.

Jeremiah A. Wright Jr. *Africans Who Shape Our Faith.* Urban Ministries, Chicago, IL, 1995.

Christianity Today. *"Churches Wary of Inner-city Islamic Inroads."* Jan. 10, 1994.

Project Joseph, P.O Box 40486, Pasadena, CA 91114. A research firm responding to the historical and biblical challenges of the Christian church.

NOTES

NOTES

NOTES

NOTES

NOTES

NOTES

NOTES

NOTES

NOTES

NOTES

NOTES

NOTES

NOTES